— THE OFFICIAL UNITED STATES —
CIVIL RIGHTS TRAIL

What happened here changed the world.

AUTHOR **LEE SENTELL**

PRINCIPAL PHOTOGRAPHER **ART MERIPOL**

GRAPHIC DESIGNER **MILES WRIGHT**

EDITOR **GLENN T. ESKEW, PH.D.**

PROJECT DIRECTOR **ED MIZZELL**

COPY EDITOR **SHARI WIMBERLY**

PRODUCTION MANAGER **LIZZIE HOLT**

PUBLISHER **ALABAMA MEDIA GROUP**

PHOTOGRAPHY CREDITS

ALL PHOTOGRAPHY ©Art Meripol unless noted

Page 4: Congressional Gold Medal, United States Mint; designer, Phebe Hemphill. Page 6: Ted Debro. Page 8: Ethan Miller/Getty Images. Page 9: Icon Sportswire/Contributor/Getty Images. Page 10: Stephen F. Somerstein/Getty Images. **TIMELINE.** Page 11: Frank M. Johnson Jr. Federal Courthouse, courtesy of the Frank M. Johnson Jr. Federal Courthouse. **LANDMARKS.** Page 16: Frank M. Johnson Jr. Federal Courthouse, courtesy of the Frank M. Johnson Jr. Federal Courthouse. Page 17: Mosaic Templars Cultural Center, courtesy of the Little Rock CVB. Harry T. & Harriette V. Moore Memorial Park & Museum, courtesy of Florida's Space Coast Office of Tourism. Bay County Courthouse, Gideon vs. Wainwright Historical Marker, courtesy of the Panama City CVB. Accord Freedom Trail, courtesy of the St. Augustine CVB. Historic Dodgertown, courtesy of Indian River County Tourism. Page 18: Albany Civil Rights Movement Museum at Old Mount Zion, courtesy of the Albany Civil Rights Movement Museum at Old Mount Zion. APEX Museum, courtesy of the APEX Museum. The Jimmy Carter Presidential Library and Museum, courtesy of The Jimmy Carter Presidential Library and Museum. Muhammad Ali Center, courtesy of the Muhammad Ali Center. SEEK Museum, courtesy of the SEEK Museum. Page 19: Southern University and A&M College, courtesy of Southern University and A&M College. Tougaloo College, courtesy of Tougaloo College. Page 20: Old Courthouse, courtesy of the Gateway Arch Park Foundation. Emanuel AME Church, John Hunter. Modjeska Monteith Simkins House, courtesy of the Modjeska Monteith Simkins House. Penn Center, courtesy of the Penn Center. Historic Liberty Hill AME Church, courtesy of Historic Liberty Hill AME Church. Page 21: Clinton 12 Statue at Green McAdoo Cultural Center, courtesy of the Green McAdoo Cultural Center. WDIA Radio Station, courtesy of the Memphis CVB. Harpers Ferry National Historical Park, courtesy of Harpers Ferry National Historical Park. **FARMVILLE.** Page 26: Bettman/Contributor/Getty Images. Page 27: Hank Walker/The LIFE Picture Collection via Getty Images. **TOPEKA.** Page 30: United States Mint; designer, Charles L. Vickers. Page 31: Carl Iwasaki/The LIFE Images Collection via Getty Images. **SUMNER.** Page 34: Bettmann/Contributor/Getty Images. Page 35: Ed Clark/The LIFE Picture Collection via Getty Images. Page 36: Tallahatchie County Courthouse, Ed Clark/The LIFE Picture Collection via Getty Images. **MONTGOMERY.** Page 40: Universal History Archive/Getty Images. Page 41: Don Cravens/The LIFE Images Collection via Getty Images. Page 42: Charles Shaw/Getty Images. Page 44: Human Pictures/Equal Justice Initiative. Page 47: Courtesy of the Rosa Parks Museum. **LITTLE ROCK.** Page 48: Afro American Newspapers/Gado/Getty Images. Page 49: Bettmann/Contributor/Getty Images. Page 50: Rolls Press/Popperfoto via Getty Images. Page 52: Bettmann/Contributor/Getty Images. **GREENSBORO.** Page 56: Donald Uhrbrock/The LIFE Images Collection via Getty Images. Page 57: Bettmann via Getty Images. Page 58: Bettmann/Contributor/Getty Images. Page 60: New York World-Telegram and The Sun Newspaper Photograph Collection, Library of Congress, Prints and Photographs Division, LC-USZ62-90145. Page 62: Keenan Hairston/GRCVB. **NASHVILLE.** Page 64: Steve Schapiro/Corbis via Getty Images. Page 65: Jimmy Ellis/*The Tennessean*. Page 66: Pin, Collection of the Smithsonian National Museum of African American History and Culture. Photo, Jack Corn/*The Tennessean*. **NEW ORLEANS.** Page 70: Bettmann/Contributor/Getty Images. Page 71: Bettmann/Contributor/Getty Images. Page 72: Artwork Courtesy of and Approved by the Norman Rockwell Family Agency. **BIRMINGHAM.** Page 74: Birmingham Police Department. Page 75: Bill Hudson/Associated Press. Page 76: Demonstrators at Kelly Ingram Park, Bill Hudson/Associated Press. Page 79: Associated Press. **JACKSON.** Page 84: Hulton Archive/Stringer/Getty Images. Page 85: New York World-Telegram and The Sun Newspaper Photograph Collection, Library of Congress, Prints and Photographs Division, LC-USZ62-135504. Page 86: Pin, Collection of the Smithsonian National Museum of African American History and Culture. Flyer, Mississippi Department of Archives & History. **WASHINGTON, D.C.** Page 90: Collection of the Smithsonian National Museum of African American History and Culture, gift of Samuel Y. Edgerton. Page 91: CNP/Getty Images. Page 92: Collection of the Smithsonian National Museum of African American History and Culture, gift of Arthur J. "Bud" Schmidt. Page 94: Bob Adelman/Corbis. Page 97: All courtesy of the Smithsonian National Museum of African American History and Culture. Top Left, Alan Karchmer. Top Right, Alan Karchmer. Bottom, Eric Long. **SELMA.** Page 100: Family photo from Cordelia Heard Billingsley. Page 101: Associated Press. Page 102: Courtesy of the Frank M. Johnson Jr. Federal Courthouse. Page 104: Flip Schulke/Corbis/Getty Images. Page 108: Pete Souza/White House. Page 109: Doug Mills/*The New York Times*. **MEMPHIS.** Page 110: Collection of the Smithsonian National Museum of African American History and Culture, gift of Arthur J. "Bud" Schmidt. Page 111: Joseph Louw/The LIFE Images Collection via Getty Images. Page 112: Collection of the Smithsonian National Museum of African American History and Culture, gift of Arthur J. "Bud" Schmidt. Page 113: Bettmann/Contributor/Getty Images. **ATLANTA.** Page 118: Flip Schulke/Corbis via Getty Images. Page 119: Flip Schulke/Corbis via Getty Images. Page 120: Donald Uhrbrock/The LIFE Images Collection via Getty Images. Page 124: Dan Cosgrove. **HISTORY.** Page 126: James Karales, LOOK Magazine Photograph Collection, Library of Congress, Prints and Photographs Division, LC-US2C4-4914. Page 127: Courtesy of Lee Sentell. Page 128: Courtesy of Lee Sentell. **BACK COVER.** Background, Warren K. Leffler. King, Flip Schulke/Corbis via Getty Images. Lewis, Steve Schapiro/Corbis via Getty Images. Obama, Pete Souza/White House. Harris, Ethan Miller/Getty Images.

THE OFFICIAL UNITED STATES CIVIL RIGHTS TRAIL:
What happened here changed the world.

Copyright © 2021 Alabama Media Group

All rights reserved. Reviewers and writers of magazine and newspaper articles may quote from this book, with attribution, as needed for their work. Otherwise, no part of this book may be reproduced or transmitted in any form or by any means, electronic or mechanical, including photocopying, recording or by any information storage and retrieval system, without written permission of the publisher.

First Edition

Printed in Canada

ISBN 978-1-57571-993-1

civilrightstrail.com

To order copies of this book, please contact:
Bart Thau, Alabama Media Group, 1731 First Ave. N., Birmingham, AL 35203; 205-325-3303

TABLE OF CONTENTS

Welcome	5	Little Rock, Arkansas	48
President Joe Biden	6	Greensboro, North Carolina	56
Vice President Kamala Harris	8	Nashville, Tennessee	64
Timeline	10	New Orleans, Louisiana	70
Landmarks	14	Birmingham, Alabama	74
Map	22	Jackson, Mississippi	84
Destinations	24	Washington, D.C.	90
Farmville, Virginia	26	Selma, Alabama	100
Topeka, Kansas	30	Memphis, Tennessee	110
Sumner, Mississippi	34	Atlanta, Georgia	118
Montgomery, Alabama	40	History of the Trail	126

The Tuskegee Airmen National Historic Site in Tuskegee, Alabama, honors the first African American military aviators in U.S. history.

Welcome to the U.S. Civil Rights Trail

The U.S. Civil Rights Trail is a collection of churches, courthouses, schools, museums and other landmarks in the American South and beyond where fearless activists played pivotal roles in advancing social justice in the 1950s and 1960s. It was the movement that changed America.

State tourism departments encourage you to follow in the footsteps of a courageous generation that was not satisfied living lives of second-class citizenship. They put their bodies, families, homes and livelihoods at risk, and bravely, slowly dismantled America's legal system of Jim Crow White supremacy. Their struggles offered hope that their children could experience Thomas Jefferson's promise in the Declaration of Independence that "all men are created equal." They successfully fought for the right to vote. Within two generations, they would even help elect a Black man as president and a Black woman as vice president.

Visit places where battles for the soul of America raged. Begin at anchors such as the National Civil Rights Museum in Memphis, where the dream of Dr. Martin Luther King Jr. lives on; the Mississippi Civil Rights Museum in Jackson, where Fannie Lou Hamer's resolve is alive; the Birmingham Civil Rights Institute, where the voice of pastor Fred Shuttlesworth still thunders; and the Martin Luther King Jr. National Historical Park in Atlanta, where his spirit remains a beacon.

Fourteen cities from Topeka to Washington, D.C., profiled in this book are home to Civil Rights Movement landmarks where African Americans fought for a better life for all people.

Visit the many sites along the trail and take pride in America's collective progress.

What happened here changed the world.

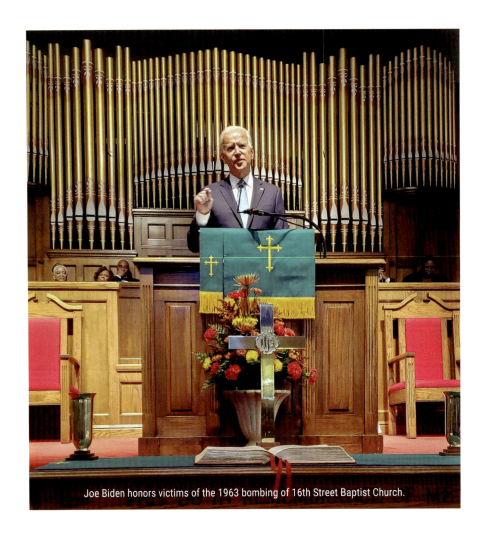

Joe Biden honors victims of the 1963 bombing of 16th Street Baptist Church.

PRESIDENT JOE BIDEN

'I'll always have your back.'

Joseph Biden, the future 46th president of the United States, stood before the packed congregation inside 16th Street Baptist Church and paid tribute to four young girls who perished when members of the Birmingham Ku Klux Klan dynamited the church on Youth Sunday. Biden spoke on the 56th anniversary of the tragic event.

"The assassination of four bright, promising, innocent young girls preparing for Sunday school, the indiscriminate cruelty of a stick of dynamite. The appalling impunity afforded the murderers while a grieving community cried out for justice and the nation watched. It pierced us," Biden said. "Addie Mae, Cynthia, Carole, Denise – their murders laid bare the lie that a child could be free in America while oppression's long shadow darkened our cities and ruled our countryside …

"I'm sure, in the first hours after the bomb exploded, it was hard to see through the smoke and rubble of this church and our hearts, hard to see through the smoke and rubble to a day like today," Biden continued. "As Dr. King eulogized those girls, perhaps not even he could have imagined that a day nearly 50 years later when the nation's first Black president would award the Congressional Gold Medal – one of our highest civilian honors – to those young women. It's only with persistent effort, it's only with fortitude, it's only with faith in ourselves and the future that may yet to be that can change things, that change comes – sometimes slowly, sometimes all at once – but it continues."

Biden concluded his remarks at the service, saying, "My prayer to all of us this morning is that in this moment when our nation must again once decide who we are, what we stand for, we will remember the strength of this community, remember the moment that time stopped, and then remember everything that came after and will choose once more to fight for our shared American dream."

Less than 500 days later, on Saturday, Nov. 7, 2020, after CNN, NBC, *The New York Times* and *The Washington Post* announced that Democrats Joe Biden and Kamala Harris had been elected president and vice president of the United States, hundreds of thousands of Americans spontaneously streamed into downtown streets across the nation in jubilation. The winners mounted a stage in Delaware that evening, and President-elect Biden thanked African Americans for their major role in the victory. The following excerpts are from his address.

"I'll have the honor of serving with a fantastic vice president … Kamala Harris, who makes history as the first woman, first Black woman, the first woman from South Asian descent, the first daughter of immigrants ever elected to this country. Don't tell me it's not possible in the United States. It's long overdue. And we're reminded tonight of those who fought so hard for so many years to make this happen. Once again, America's bent the arc of the moral universe more toward justice … When this campaign was at its lowest ebb, the African American community stood up again for me. You've always had my back, and I'll have yours …

"America has called upon us to marshal the forces of decency, the forces of fairness. To marshal the forces of science and the forces of hope in the great battles of our time. The battle to control the virus, the battle to build prosperity, the battle to secure your family's health care. The battle to achieve racial justice and root out systemic racism in this country …

"America has always, is shaped, by inflection points, by moments in time. We've made hard decisions about who we are and what we want to be. Lincoln in 1860, coming to save the Union. FDR in 1932, promising a beleaguered country a new deal. JFK in 1960, pledging a new frontier. And 12 years ago, when Barack Obama made history, he told us, Yes, We Can … Let us be the nation that we know we can. A nation united, a nation strengthened. A nation healed. The United States of America, ladies and gentlemen, there's never, never been anything we've tried we've not been able to do."

In his inaugural address after being sworn in as president on Jan. 20, 2021, Biden continued the theme of equity and unity, saying, "A cry for racial justice some 400 years in the making moves us. The dream of justice for all will be deferred no longer."

While Kamala Harris may be the first female vice president, she asserts, "I won't be the last."

VICE PRESIDENT KAMALA HARRIS

Women: 'The Backbone of Democracy'

Kamala Harris – former California attorney general, former U.S. senator and now vice president – launched her presidential bid in early 2019 as the nation observed what would have been the 90th birthday of civil rights leader Dr. Martin Luther King Jr. During her campaign, she often remarked that she had had a "stroller's-eye view" of the Civil Rights Movement because her parents had wheeled her and her sister, Maya, to protests. The daughter of a Jamaican father and an Indian mother, Harris notes that she is both African American and Indian American and also "a proud American."

Two months into her campaign, her platform of raising teacher salaries earned her endorsements from prominent Black legislators in South Carolina. This support was significant since the state was hosting the first Democratic primary in the South. Harris impressed veteran South Carolina Sen. Darrell Jackson, pastor of Bible Way Church in Columbia, one of the state's largest and most influential African American congregations. State Rep. JA Moore, a small-business owner whose sister was among the nine churchgoers slain in the 2015 Charleston shooting massacre, backed Harris because he saw her as a fighter capable of taking on the incumbent president. "She has a record of standing up to bullies," Moore said.

After Harris delivered a well-received campaign address in Birmingham, Alabama, in June of that year, audience members speculated that Democrats would nominate a Biden-Harris ticket. Her campaign ended before New Year's Day 2020, but South Carolina had indeed played an outsized role in determining the Democratic nominee. Powerful U.S. Rep. James E. Clyburn endorsed Joe Biden the weekend before the state's Feb. 29 primary. As a result, Biden captured 49 percent of the state's primary vote to Bernie Sanders' 20 percent. Other candidates soon dropped out of the race.

On Aug. 11, 2020, presidential nominee Joe Biden made history when he introduced Kamala Harris to the world as potentially America's first female and first person of color as vice president. More than 81 million voters agreed with his choice, creating a White House team that more reflected the diversity of America. On an outdoor stage on Nov. 17 in Delaware, freshly minted Vice President-elect Kamala Harris, dressed in suffragette white, quoted her late friend U.S. Rep. John Lewis, saying, " 'Democracy is not a state. It is an act.' And what he meant was that America's democracy is not guaranteed. It is only as strong as our willingness to fight for it, to guard it and never take it for granted. And protecting our democracy takes struggle." She also referenced her mother's experience of coming to the U.S. from India at the age of 19. "Maybe she didn't quite imagine this moment. But she believed so deeply in an America where a moment like this is possible," Harris said. "So, I'm thinking about her and about the generations of women – Black women, Asian, White, Latina and Native American women throughout our nation's history – who have paved the way for this moment tonight. Women who fought and sacrificed so much for equality, liberty and justice for all, including the Black women, who are too often overlooked but so often prove that they are the backbone of our democracy."

Harris acknowledged the women who had worked to secure and protect the right to vote for over a century, from the passage of the 19th Amendment, to the Voting Rights Act, to the new generation of women casting ballots. "Tonight, I reflect on their struggle, their determination and the strength of their vision – to see what can be unburdened by what has been – I stand on their shoulders," she said. "And what a testament it is to Joe's character that he had the audacity to break one of the most substantial barriers that exists in our country and select a woman as his vice president. But while I may be the first woman in this office, I won't be the last. Because every little girl watching tonight sees that this is a country of possibilities."

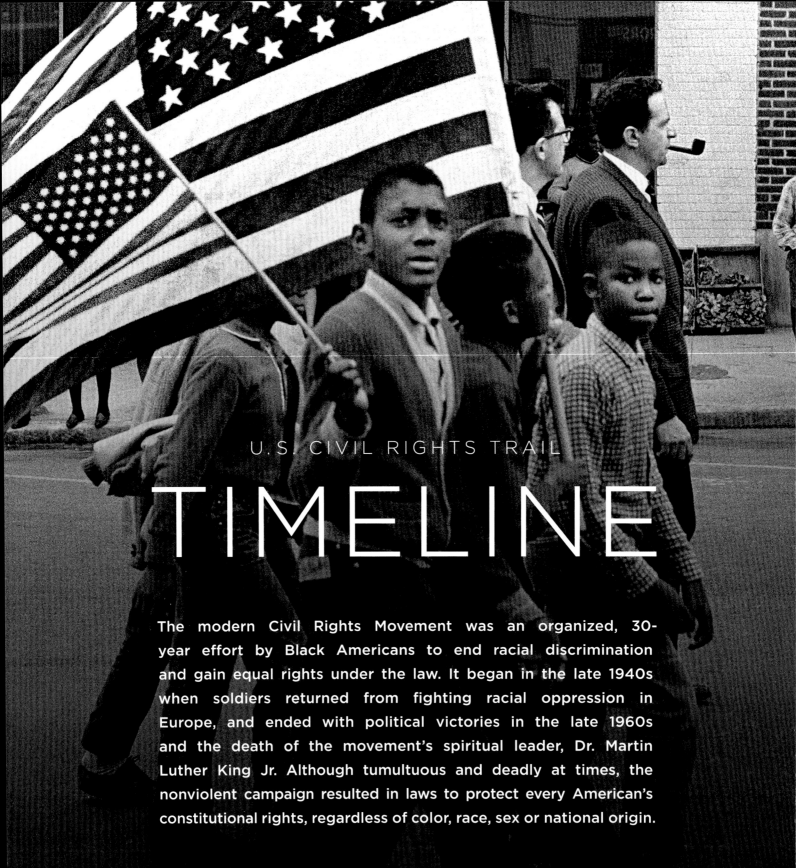

U.S. CIVIL RIGHTS TRAIL

TIMELINE

The modern Civil Rights Movement was an organized, 30-year effort by Black Americans to end racial discrimination and gain equal rights under the law. It began in the late 1940s when soldiers returned from fighting racial oppression in Europe, and ended with political victories in the late 1960s and the death of the movement's spiritual leader, Dr. Martin Luther King Jr. Although tumultuous and deadly at times, the nonviolent campaign resulted in laws to protect every American's constitutional rights, regardless of color, race, sex or national origin.

1941-45 Black airmen trained at Moton Field in Tuskegee, Alabama, and fought for the U.S. during World War II.

July 26, 1948 President Harry Truman issued Executive Order 9981 to end segregation in the military.

December 1, 1955 Rosa Parks refused to give up her seat to boarding White passengers on a Montgomery bus. Threatened with arrest, she replied, "You may do that." Her cool but defiant stance prompted a yearlong bus boycott led by 26-year-old pastor Martin Luther King Jr. The boycott ended when the U.S. Supreme Court voided laws that permitted racial segregation on public transportation.

May 17, 1954 With its decision on *Brown v. Board of Education of Topeka*, a consolidation of five cases into one, the U.S. Supreme Court led by Chief Justice Earl Warren effectively ended 60 years of official racial segregation in public schools. Many schools, however, remained segregated, and Jim Crow laws remained in force for years throughout the South.

September 4, 1957 The Arkansas National Guard blocked African American students known as the Little Rock Nine from integrating Central High School. To enforce the court's ruling, President Dwight D. Eisenhower sent federal troops to escort the students who nevertheless continued to be harassed by White classmates and city residents.

December 20, 1956 The Montgomery Bus Boycott ended after 12 months.

September 9, 1957 Eisenhower signed into law the Civil Rights Act of 1957, which protected voting rights by allowing federal prosecution of officials who suppressed another person's right to vote.

| PRE-1954 | 1954 | 1955 | 1956 | 1957 | 1958 |

May 14, 1954 The Rev. Martin Luther King Jr. moved to Montgomery, Alabama, and became pastor of Dexter Avenue Baptist Church.

August 28, 1955 White supremacists brutally murdered Emmett Till, a 14-year-old Chicago youth visiting relatives in Mississippi, for allegedly offending a White woman in her rural store. *Jet* magazine published gruesome photos of the boy's battered body at his open-casket funeral, stunning people around the world who called for social justice for African Americans. A court later acquitted Emmett's murderers.

June 5, 1956 Citing the precedent of the *Brown* decision, the U.S. District Court in Alabama led by Judge Frank M. Johnson Jr. struck down — in *Browder v. Gayle* — Montgomery's segregated seating that required Black people to sit in the back of the bus.

November 13, 1956 The U.S. Supreme Court affirmed the application of the *Brown* decision to other forms of segregation and upheld the Alabama District Court ruling in *Browder v. Gayle* that had ordered the desegregation of public transportation.

December 25, 1956 The home of the Rev. Fred Shuttlesworth, civil rights leader and pastor of Bethel Baptist Church, was bombed in Birmingham, Alabama.

1958 Howard University law student Bruce Boynton of Selma, Alabama, challenged his arrest for "trespassing" and violating segregation in a Richmond bus station café. In 1960, the *Boynton v. Virginia* case appeared before the Supreme Court, which ruled for desegregation in interstate public transportation.

February 14, 1957 The Southern Christian Leadership Conference formally incorporated at New Zion Baptist Church in New Orleans.

February 1, 1960 Four Black college students in Greensboro, North Carolina, refused to leave a Woolworth's "Whites only" lunch counter without being served. The Greensboro Four – Ezell Blair Jr., David Richmond, Franklin McCain and Joseph McNeil – were inspired by the nonviolent protest of Mahatma Gandhi. The Greensboro Sit-In, as it came to be called, quickly sparked similar sit-ins throughout the city and in other states.

July 25, 1960 Woolworth in Greensboro integrated its lunch counter.

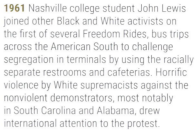

1961 Nashville college student John Lewis joined other Black and White activists on the first of several Freedom Rides, bus trips across the American South to challenge segregation in terminals by using the racially separate restrooms and cafeterias. Horrific violence by White supremacists against the nonviolent demonstrators, most notably in South Carolina and Alabama, drew international attention to the protest.

September 29, 1962 The registration of James Meredith as the first Black student to attend the University of Mississippi resulted in White supremacists attacking federal marshals and violently rioting on the Ole Miss campus.

June 11, 1963 Gov. George C. Wallace blocked two Black students from registering to attend the University of Alabama by standing in the schoolhouse door until ushered aside by federal marshals who threatened to arrest him for violating the court-ordered desegregation.

1959   1960   1961   1962   1963

May 10, 1960 The Nashville sit-in movement led by the Rev. James Lawson pressured the city to integrate lunch counters. It was the first Southern municipality to do so.

November 10, 1960 New Orleans became the first Southern city to integrate elementary schools.

November 14, 1960 Six-year-old Ruby Bridges was escorted by four armed federal marshals as she became the first student to integrate William Frantz Elementary School in New Orleans. Her bravery inspired Norman Rockwell's 1964 painting *The Problem We All Live With*.

April 3, 1963 The Rev. Fred Shuttlesworth, the Rev. Ralph David Abernathy and Dr. King launched the Birmingham Campaign with a boycott of stores during the Easter shopping season. Once protest marches began, Commissioner of Public Safety Bull Connor ordered police dogs sicced on Black bystanders and high-powered water cannon fired on nonviolent demonstrators.

April 12, 1963 Bull Connor arrested Dr. King, Abernathy and Shuttlesworth for marching. While incarcerated, Dr. King wrote "Letter from Birmingham Jail."

June 12, 1963 NAACP field secretary Medgar Evers was shot and killed in front of his Jackson, Mississippi, home.

August 28, 1963 Approximately 250,000 people took part in the March on Washington for Jobs and Freedom. Dr. King delivered his "I Have a Dream" speech in front of the Lincoln Memorial, stating, "I have a dream that one day this nation will rise up and live out the true meaning of its creed: 'We hold these truths to be self-evident: that all men are created equal.'"

March 7, 1965 Alabama state troopers and local deputies brutally attacked 600 voting-rights advocates when they reached the foot of Selma's Edmund Pettus Bridge on their way to the state Capitol in Montgomery. Worldwide condemnation followed international media coverage of "Bloody Sunday."

November 22, 1963 President John F. Kennedy was assassinated.

March 25, 1965 The Selma-to-Montgomery March concluded with Dr. King's delivering his "How Long, Not Long" speech at the Alabama Capitol before an audience of 25,000 people.

August 30, 1967 Thurgood Marshall became the first African American justice of the U.S. Supreme Court.

1964   1965   1966   1967   1968   1969

August 6, 1965 In a quick reaction to the Bloody Sunday violence, Congress passed and President Johnson signed the Voting Rights Act of 1965 to prevent the use of literacy tests as a voting requirement. It also allowed federal examiners to review voter qualifications and federal observers to monitor polling places.

April 11, 1968 President Johnson signed the Civil Rights Act of 1968, also known as the Fair Housing Act, providing equal housing opportunity regardless of race, religion or national origin.

September 15, 1963 The Ku Klux Klan tried to stop school desegregation by exploding a dynamite bomb at 16th Street Baptist Church in Birmingham that killed four young Black girls and injured dozens more people before Sunday services. The international media registered the world's outrage over the murders.

October 14, 1964 Dr. King received the Nobel Peace Prize.

April 4, 1968 An assassin shot Dr. King in Memphis where he had gone at the request of the Rev. James Lawson to support striking garbage collectors. The effort was to be an example of the Poor People's Campaign set to occupy Washington, D.C., later that month and demand economic justice.

July 2, 1964 Buoyed by national pressure following the violence against civil rights demonstrators the previous year in Birmingham, President Lyndon B. Johnson signed the Civil Rights Act of 1964 into law. It prevented employment discrimination due to race, color, sex, religion or national origin. A section established the U.S. Equal Employment Opportunity Commission (EEOC) to help prevent workplace discrimination.

Contributing: History.com

U.S. CIVIL RIGHTS TRAIL

LANDMARKS

ALABAMA

Anniston
Freedom Riders National Monument

Birmingham
16th Street Baptist Church
Bethel Baptist Church
Birmingham Civil Rights Institute
Kelly Ingram Park

Monroeville
Old Courthouse Museum

Montgomery
Alabama Capitol
City of St. Jude
Civil Rights Memorial Center
Dexter Avenue King Memorial Baptist Church
Dexter Parsonage Museum
First Baptist Church (Ripley Street)
Frank M. Johnson Jr. Federal Building and United States Courthouse
Freedom Rides Museum
Holt Street Baptist Church
Montgomery Interpretive Center

Rosa Parks Museum
The Legacy Museum
The National Memorial for Peace and Justice

Scottsboro
The Scottsboro Boys Museum and Cultural Center

Selma
Brown Chapel AME Church
Edmund Pettus Bridge
Lowndes Interpretive Center
National Voting Rights Museum and Institute
Selma Interpretive Center
Selma to Montgomery National Historic Trail

Tuscaloosa
Foster Auditorium at the University of Alabama

Tuskegee
Butler Chapel AME Zion Church
Tuskegee Airmen National Historic Site
Tuskegee History Center
Tuskegee University

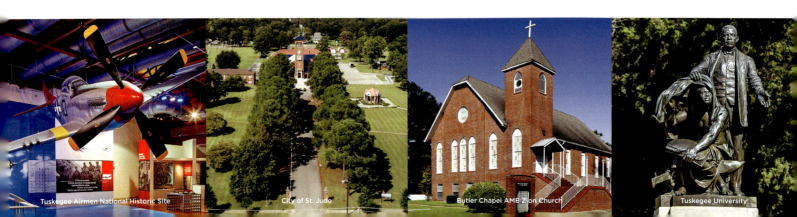

ARKANSAS

Little Rock

Arkansas Civil Rights Heritage Trail

Clinton Presidential Center

Daisy Bates House

Little Rock Central High School National Historic Site

Little Rock Nine Memorial

Mosaic Templars Cultural Center

DELAWARE

Wilmington

Howard High School of Technology

DISTRICT OF COLUMBIA

Washington

Howard University: Andrew Rankin Memorial Chapel, Frederick Douglass Memorial Hall, Founders Library

John Philip Sousa Middle School

Lincoln Memorial

Martin Luther King Jr. Memorial

National Museum of African American History and Culture

Supreme Court of the United States

FLORIDA

Mims

Harry T. & Harriette V. Moore Memorial Park & Museum

Panama City

Bay County Courthouse, Gideon v. Wainwright Historical Marker

Sarasota

Newtown African American History Trail

St. Augustine

Accord Freedom Trail

Vero Beach

Historic Dodgertown

GEORGIA

Albany
Albany Civil Rights Movement Museum at Old Mount Zion

Shiloh Baptist Church

Atlanta
APEX Museum

Ebenezer Baptist Church

Elbert P. Tuttle United States Court of Appeals Building

Martin Luther King Jr. Birth Home

Martin Luther King Jr. National Historical Park

National Center for Civil and Human Rights

The Jimmy Carter Presidential Library and Museum

The King Center

Midway
Dorchester Academy Boys' Dormitory

KANSAS

Topeka
Brown v. Board of Education National Historic Site

Sumner Elementary School

KENTUCKY

Berea
Lincoln Hall at Berea College

Louisville
Louisville Downtown Civil Rights Trail

Muhammad Ali Center

Russellville
SEEK Museum

Simpsonville
Whitney M. Young Jr. Birthplace

LOUISIANA

Baton Rouge
Louisiana Capitol
Southern University and A&M College

New Orleans
5th Circuit Court of Appeals
New Zion Baptist Church
Tremé Neighborhood
William Frantz Elementary School

MISSISSIPPI

Canton
Canton Freedom House Civil Rights Museum

Glendora
Emmett Till Historic Intrepid Center

Jackson
Medgar and Myrlie Evers Home National Monument
Mississippi Civil Rights Museum
Mississippi Freedom Trail
Tougaloo College

Money
Bryant's Grocery & Meat Market

Oxford
Lyceum – The Circle Historic District, University of Mississippi

Philadelphia
Neshoba County Historic Sites

Ruleville
Fannie Lou Hamer Memorial Statue

Sumner
Emmett Till Interpretive Center
Tallahatchie County Courthouse

MISSOURI

Independence
Harry S. Truman Presidential Library & Museum

St. Louis
Old Courthouse
Shelley House

NORTH CAROLINA

Durham
Hayti Heritage Center

Greensboro
February One Monument
International Civil Rights Center & Museum (F.W. Woolworth Building)

Raleigh
Dr. Martin Luther King Jr. Memorial Gardens
Estey Hall at Shaw University

SOUTH CAROLINA

Charleston
Emanuel AME Church

Columbia
Modjeska Monteith Simkins House
South Carolina State House

Greenville
Springfield Baptist Church

Greenwood
Benjamin E. Mays House Museum

Orangeburg
Orangeburg Massacre

Rock Hill
McCrory's

St. Helena Island
Penn Center (formerly Penn School)

Summerton
Historic Liberty Hill AME Church

TENNESSEE

Clinton

Clinton 12 Statue at Green McAdoo Cultural Center

Memphis

Beale Street Historic District

Clayborn Temple

Mason Temple Church of God in Christ

National Civil Rights Museum at the Lorraine Motel

WDIA Radio Station

Nashville

Civil Rights Room at the Nashville Public Library

Clark Memorial United Methodist Church

Davidson County Courthouse and *Witness Walls*

Fifth Avenue Historic District

Fisk University

Griggs Hall at American Baptist College

VIRGINIA

Farmville

Robert Russa Moton High School and Museum

Richmond

Virginia Civil Rights Memorial

WEST VIRGINIA

Charleston

Elizabeth Harden Gilmore House

Harpers Ferry

Harpers Ferry National Historical Park

Huntington

Memphis Tennessee Garrison House

FARMVILLE, VIRGINIA

TOPEKA, KANSAS

SUMNER, MISSISSIPPI

MONTGOMERY, ALABAMA

LITTLE ROCK, ARKANSAS

GREENSBORO, NORTH CAROLINA

NASHVILLE, TENNESSEE

NEW ORLEANS, LOUISIANA

BIRMINGHAM, ALABAMA

JACKSON, MISSISSIPPI

WASHINGTON,
DISTRICT OF COLUMBIA

SELMA, ALABAMA

MEMPHIS, TENNESSEE

ATLANTA, GEORGIA

**MORE THAN 100 LOCATIONS
ACROSS 15 STATES**

U.S. CIVIL RIGHTS TRAIL

DESTINATIONS

1951

FARMVILLE
VIRGINIA

When the U.S. Supreme Court ruled in *Plessy v. Ferguson* in 1896 that "separate but equal" public facilities were legal, racial segregation became the law of the land for more than half a century. In 1954, the high court overturned *Plessy* in the landmark decision *Brown v. Board of Education of Topeka* that shook the nation. The NAACP had consolidated five lawsuits into one to form the *Brown* case. These lawsuits came from Black plaintiffs in four states and the District of Columbia and challenged the legality of school segregation. A Virginia case from Farmville contributed 75 percent of the total number of plaintiffs and, most notably, was the only case triggered by students.

Robert Russa Moton High School, designed in 1939 for 180 students in Prince Edward County, overflowed in 1951 with all of the county's 477 Black high school students. Many studied in hastily constructed tar-paper classrooms that leaked when it rained. The school had no library, science lab, gymnasium or cafeteria. Sixteen-year-old Barbara Johns, whose uncle Vernon Johns was the rare Black pastor who called for equal rights from his Alabama pulpit, felt the urge for change. In hopes of getting a new school with indoor restrooms and, not incidentally, better curriculum, she led her fellow students on a walkout on April 23, 1951. Black families filed suit.

Thurgood Marshall, lead attorney for the NAACP, argued the case before the Supreme Court on which he would eventually serve. The Earl Warren-led court ruled 9-0 that separate schools could never truly be equal. After the court ordered the Virginia county to desegregate its schools, the school board responded by shutting down all 21 public schools and diverted public monies to establish private "academies" for Whites only. Meanwhile, death threats compelled Barbara Johns to move to Montgomery, Alabama, to live with relatives for her safety. For five years, many of Prince Edward County's Black students had no access to educational training and some never recovered.

After Moton High School closed in 1993, the Martha E. Forrester Council of Women purchased the building and saved it from demolition. The National Park Service opened the Robert Russa Moton Museum in 2003. Declared a National Historic Landmark, the site honors the birthplace of America's student-led civil rights revolution.

Thurgood Marshall

A student-led strike at Robert Russa Moton High School began as a demand for improved facilities but led to the integration of Prince Edward County public schools.

ROBERT RUSSA MOTON HIGH SCHOOL & MUSEUM

In the 1940s, Robert Russa Moton High School housed 450 African American students in a space built for only 180. When it rained, students had to use umbrellas inside to stay dry. A National Historic Landmark, the school was turned into a museum commemorating the walkout led by students Barbara Johns and John Arthur Stokes.

Barbara Johns, a leader of the student walkout in Farmville, is prominently featured in the Virginia Civil Rights Memorial on the grounds of the Capitol in Richmond.

1954

TOPEKA
KANSAS

Across the South, Black parents wanted their children to receive a great education in order to succeed in life, but local school boards spent only a fraction on building, staffing and operating facilities for Black students as compared to those for Whites. After the Great Depression and World War II, Black parents challenged their local school systems. Some wanted their children to attend the better funded White schools while others just wanted equal Black schools. By the early 1950s, the NAACP compiled cases to demonstrate the inequalities and to challenge segregation laws in public education. The organization filed lawsuits on behalf of Black plaintiffs in several Southern states.

In 1947, South Carolina's Clarendon County school system operated a fleet of 33 buses that shuttled White children to school. No buses carried the county's Black students, many of whom were forced to walk for miles to and from school every day. When Black parents petitioned the Clarendon County School Board, asking for transportation for their children, they were ignored. Harry and Eliza Briggs were among the 20 parents who then filed a lawsuit against the school board, challenging segregation. The South Carolina case is notable in part because of testimony by psychologists Mamie and Kenneth Clark, a husband-and-wife team, who studied children's racial biases. In experiments, the Clarks allowed Black children to choose either White dolls or Black dolls to play with. A majority of Black children showed a preference for dolls with White skin, a consequence of the negative effects of segregation, the Clarks argued.

After the eventual court decision in 1954, many of the South Carolina plaintiffs lost their jobs. In 2004, U.S. Rep. James E. Clyburn and Sen. Fritz Hollings earned approval for a Congressional Gold Medal of Honor to be posthumously awarded to Harry and Eliza Briggs, the Rev. Joseph A. DeLaine, who was a school principal, and Levi Pearson, a local farmer, for their courage in the fight for educational equality in Clarendon County. It was the only such action associated with the *Brown v. Board of Education* case.

In Wilmington County, Delaware, Sarah Bulah and Ethel Belton were upset that their children had to bypass White schools to reach

Congressional Gold Medal of Honor presented to Harry and Eliza Briggs, the Rev. Joseph A. DeLaine and Levi Pearson

Student Linda Brown, whose father was a plaintiff in the *Brown vs. Board of Education of Topeka* case, attended the segregated Monroe Elementary School.

Black ones and sought to challenge state-enforced segregation. A state court ruled in their favor. An appeal to the Delaware Supreme Court and the U.S. Supreme Court followed. And in rural Virginia, a courageous 16-year-old Barbara Johns led schoolmates in a walkout on April 23, 1951, in hopes of getting a building more adequate for their needs. It did not end well for the Prince Edward County students. Even after the Supreme Court ruled in 1954 that separate education facilities were "inherently unequal," the county responded by closing all county schools for five years while building White "academies" with public funds, leaving many Black students with no options for education.

In 1951 in what became the *Brown* case's namesake, the NAACP filed a class-action suit in Oliver Brown's name against the Board of Education of Topeka after his daughter Linda Brown and her Black classmates were denied entrance to an all-White elementary school a short walk from their homes. When Brown's case, the three others detailed here and a school-segregation case from the District of Columbia first went before the Supreme Court in 1952, the court combined them into a single case under the name *Brown v. Board of Education of Topeka*. Early on, the justices were divided on how to rule on school segregation, with Chief Justice Fred M. Vinson holding the opinion that the 1896 *Plessy v. Ferguson* "separate but equal" verdict should stand. But in the fall of 1953, before *Brown* was to be heard, Vinson died. President Dwight D. Eisenhower filled the vacancy with Earl Warren, the widely respected third-term governor of California who had been the Republican vice presidential nominee with Thomas Dewey in 1948.

Thurgood Marshall, head of the NAACP Legal Defense and Educational Fund and an honors graduate of Howard University School of Law, served as the chief attorney for the Black plaintiffs. Marshall argued that schools for Black children were not equal to White schools and that segregation violated the Equal Protection Clause of the 14th Amendment. It holds that no state can "deny to any person within its jurisdiction the equal protection of the laws." Displaying considerable political skill and determination, Chief Justice Warren succeeded in only 10 weeks on the bench in crafting a unanimous opinion that invalidated racial segregation in public schools.

In the decision, issued on May 17, 1954, Warren wrote that "in the field of public education the doctrine of 'separate but equal' has no place," as segregated schools are "inherently unequal." As a result, the court ruled that the plaintiffs were being "deprived of the equal protection of the laws guaranteed by the 14th Amendment." Segregationists termed the date "Black Monday" and vowed massive resistance across the South. It took decades for some states and counties to comply and end Jim Crow practices in schools.

Beyond desegregating public education, the *Brown* precedent eventually spread to numerous fields where segregation had hindered the advancement of Black Americans. Thirteen years after the *Brown* decision, President Lyndon Johnson appointed Marshall as the nation's first Black Supreme Court justice. He served with distinction for 24 years.

Pin supporting equal educational opportunities

BROWN V. BOARD OF EDUCATION NATIONAL HISTORIC SITE

This site commemorates the historic U.S. Supreme Court decision that changed America forever: *Brown v. Board of Education of Topeka*. The children of three plaintiffs in the case attended Monroe Elementary School, one of four elementary schools for Black students in Topeka. The restored school was purchased by the National Park Service and reopened in 2004 as a National Historic Site and civil rights interpretive center.

1955

SUMNER
MISSISSIPPI

Chicago resident Mamie Till Bradley packed her 14-year-old son's bags in August 1955 for a visit with relatives in Mississippi in the wake of the U.S. Supreme Court's *Brown v. Board of Education of Topeka* decision. She could not have imagined that he would not return alive. The heartbroken mother chose an open-casket funeral in Chicago, wanting to show the world the atrocities committed against her child. Thousands of mourners came to pay their respects. *Jet* magazine published photographs of the distraught mother viewing her son's body along with images of his tortured face, which generated widespread outrage that fueled civil rights protests.

White supremacists had murdered the teenager after he had allegedly "wolf-whistled" at Carolyn Bryant, the White storekeeper who sold him candy at Bryant's Grocery in rural Money. Three nights later, on Aug. 28, her husband, Roy Bryant, and his half-brother J.W. Milam kidnapped Emmett from the home of his great-uncle Mose Wright. They – and others – beat and tortured the boy for hours before killing him with a bullet to the head.

The killers then attached a 75-pound cotton gin fan to his neck with barbed wire before dumping his body into the Tallahatchie River.

After the body resurfaced, Bryant and Milam stood trial for murder in the small town of Sumner in September. The drama in the packed courtroom in the Tallahatchie County Courthouse attracted substantial national media, irritating locals. Even though Emmett's great-uncle bravely identified Milam and Bryant as the men who had abducted his nephew at gunpoint, the all-White jury returned a not-guilty verdict after deliberating about an hour.

In 1956, Southern journalist William Bradford Huie paid Milam and Bryant $3,150 for admitting guilt in a controversial article printed in *Look* magazine. Decades later, Duke University historian Tim Tyson quoted Emmett's accuser, Carolyn Bryant Donham, in the best-selling book *The Blood of Emmett Till*. She admitted that some of her accusations against the boy "never happened," adding, "Nothing that boy did justified what happened to him."

Emmett Till

The murder trial of 14-year-old Emmett Till exposed the racial injustice prevalent in the Deep South.

County leaders issued a formal apology for the injustices to the Till family in 2007. This followed the formation of the Emmett Till Memorial Commission a year earlier. Jerome G. Little, the first African American president of the Tallahatchie County Board of Supervisors, established the 501(c)(3) organization, which worked to restore the courthouse to its appearance during the 1955 trial and to create the Emmett Till Interpretive Center. The museum exists to tell the story of the Till tragedy and show the way to racial reconciliation. Most recently, the commission partnered with Florida State University to create the Emmett Till Memory Project, an app and website that directs visitors to relevant historical sites.

In nearby Glendora, where J.W. Milam lived and ran a store, Mayor Johnny B. Thomas opened the Emmett Till Historic Intrepid Center (ETHIC) in 2005. Located in a renovated cotton gin, the ETHIC Museum features a replica façade of Bryant's Grocery and a diorama of the bedroom at Emmett's great-uncle's house from which he was kidnapped.

After the FBI reopened the case in 2004, authorities exhumed Emmett's body for an autopsy and then reburied it in a new casket at the Burr Oak Cemetery in Alsip outside Chicago. The original casket became a featured exhibit in the Smithsonian National Museum of African American History and Culture in Washington, D.C.

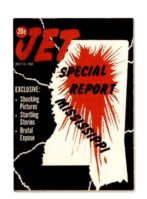

Jet magazine's Emmett Till issue, July 23, 1964

The Till murder trial, which lasted only five days, drew crowds to the Tallahatchie County Courthouse. The all-White, all-male jury returned a not-guilty verdict.

TALLAHATCHIE COUNTY COURTHOUSE & EMMETT TILL INTERPRETIVE CENTER

The Tallahatchie County Courthouse where Emmett Till's murder trial took place has been preserved as a museum, with the interpretive center across the street helping to tell the story. Visitors can book tours of the courthouse as well as the interpretive center, which uses a combination of storytelling and art to educate visitors about the tragedy of Emmett's murder and point the way toward racial healing.

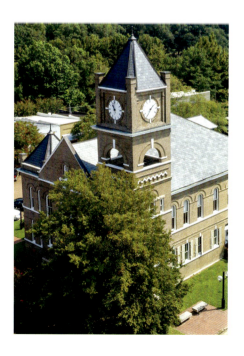

EMMETT TILL HISTORIC INTREPID CENTER

The Emmett Till Historic Intrepid Center (ETHIC) is located midway between Money and Sumner in the town of Glendora where some of Emmett's murderers lived. Housed in a converted cotton gin, the ETHIC Museum features exhibits regarding the Black youth's fateful visit to Mississippi. Nearby stretches the Tallahatchie River in which the killers threw Emmett's body, weighted down by a cotton gin fan.

BRYANT'S GROCERY & MEAT MARKET

The ruins of the Bryant's Grocery & Meat Market storefront in the community of Money are all that remain of the store itself, but a historical marker stands at the site and is part of the Mississippi Freedom Trail.

1955

MONTGOMERY
ALABAMA

Montgomery bus driver James Blake angrily told Rosa Parks that he would have her arrested if she did not yield her seat to Whites boarding at the Empire Theater bus stop. It was Thursday, Dec. 1, 1955. The 42-year-old seamstress, active with the NAACP, was upset about the horrible murder of Emmett Till three months earlier. In defiance of the city ordinance, she softly replied, "You may do that."

The next day, the 26-year-old Dr. Martin Luther King Jr., who had been pastor of Dexter Avenue Baptist Church for just 14 months, welcomed 50 Black community leaders to the basement of his church and organized a one-day boycott of city buses, similar to what pastors in Baton Rouge, Louisiana, had done two years earlier. As hoped, buses ran empty on Monday, and thousands gathered at Holt Street Baptist Church that evening and vowed to stay off buses until city leaders agreed to their modest requests: courteous treatment, equal boarding with Whites and that some Black drivers be hired. The Montgomery Improvement Association, formed to manage the boycott, gave Dr. King 20 minutes' notice that he was to be the keynote speaker that night. Fortunately for history, Dr. King's wife, Coretta Scott King, had recently given birth to daughter Yolanda and could not attend, so she asked that her husband's remarks be recorded. This was his first public speech.

Seven weeks after the launch of the successful boycott, a threatening telephone call to the Dexter parsonage at midnight shook Dr. King's faith. As he sat at the kitchen table to drink a cup of coffee and pray, an inner voice told him to stand up in support of righteousness. The voice promised to be with Dr. King forever. The young pastor later explained the revelation as his first intimate encounter with God and that it strengthened his resolve for the challenges ahead. Nights later, White supremacists exploded dynamite on his front porch in an assassination attempt that nearly killed his wife and baby. Dr. King was not home at the time. Neighbors gathered demanding revenge, but upon his return, Dr. King calmed their anger and stayed true to the principles of nonviolence under challenging circumstances.

Mug shot of Rosa Parks

At the end of the successful Montgomery Bus Boycott, Rosa Parks and others again boarded city buses.

For 381 days, Montgomery's 50,000 Black residents walked or carpooled to get to work. It was the first sustained mass defiance of segregation. Meanwhile, Parks' attorney, Fred Gray, filed suit against the city to challenge segregated public seating. The case drew national attention, and Parks and former first lady Eleanor Roosevelt raised funds on an NAACP-sponsored speaking tour that drew 20,000 people to Madison Square Garden in New York. Montgomery's U.S. District Judge Frank M. Johnson Jr. concurred with attorney Gray's position, and the U.S. Supreme Court confirmed on Nov. 13, 1956, that segregation of public transportation was unconstitutional. It was a landmark victory for the fledgling movement.

Two months after the end of the successful boycott and following a second failed assassination attempt by the Ku Klux Klan to kill the Kings at the Dexter parsonage, Dr. King told the church that because of their legal victory he could die happy because he had "been to the mountaintop and seen the promised land." Dr. King would voice similar thoughts in Memphis 11 years later on the night before his assassination. The charismatic pastor had become the most visible figure in the South's freedom movement.

Dr. King left Montgomery in 1960 and moved to his hometown of Atlanta, where he continued to lead the Southern Christian Leadership Conference (SCLC). However, in May 1961, he rushed back to the city to support injured Freedom Riders that included 21-year-old John Lewis and his college roommate Bernard Lafayette Jr. They and other Black and White protestors had been brutally beaten by the Klan outside the Greyhound bus station. Dr. King found uneasy demonstrators gathered inside First Baptist Church at 347 North Ripley Street, pastored by his best friend and fellow movement leader, the Rev. Ralph D. Abernathy. An armed White mob milled about outside burning cars and threatening to set fire to the church containing the Freedom Riders and local movement supporters. Gov. John Patterson sent in the National Guard to disperse the domestic terrorists. Months later, Abernathy, who had co-founded the SCLC, accepted the pastorate of a major church in Atlanta and joined Dr. King there.

Montgomery continued to be a stage for civil rights efforts. In early 1965, voting-rights activist Jimmie Lee Jackson died of gunshot injuries in the town of Marion at the hands of state trooper James Bonard Fowler (a crime that went unpunished for 45 years). Dr. King agreed to lead a march from Selma to Montgomery to confront the governor about this injustice. Dr. King stayed at home in Atlanta on what became known as Bloody Sunday, but he and his wife headlined the third and successful Selma-to-Montgomery march. Speaking from a flatbed truck in front of the Capitol on March 25, Dr. King told thousands of supporters who filled Dexter Avenue that he knew people were asking how long the freedom movement would take. He said it would not be long because "truth crushed to earth" will rise again. The scene was replayed a half-century later by actor David Oyelowo, who – standing behind the actual pulpit used at Dr. King's former Montgomery church – reprised the "How Long" address in Ava DuVernay's Oscar-winning movie *Selma*.

John Lewis, Dr. Martin Luther King Jr. and Coretta Scott King in front of the Alabama Capitol

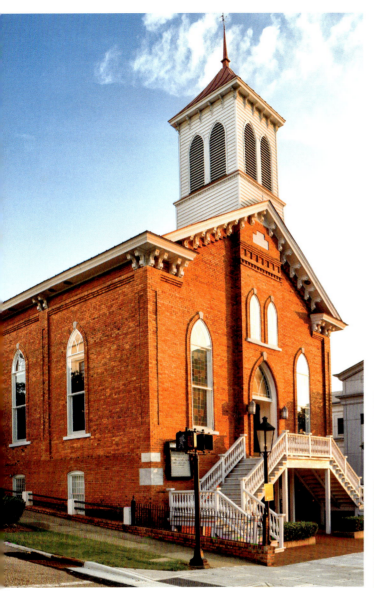

DEXTER AVENUE KING MEMORIAL BAPTIST CHURCH

Dexter Avenue Baptist Church was organized in 1877 and built between 1883 and 1889. Because of the church's association with Dr. King, who was pastor from 1954 to 1960, it was designated a National Historic Landmark in 1974. And in 2008, the Department of the Interior named it to the U.S. Tentative List for UNESCO World Heritage.

DEXTER PARSONAGE

Two months into the Montgomery Bus Boycott and three nights after "the presence of the Divine" told Dr. King to stand up for righteousness and justice, racists exploded a bomb on the porch of the Dexter Avenue Baptist Church parsonage at 309 South Jackson Street. Dr. King calmed neighbors who wanted vengeance, staying true to the principle of nonviolence under trying times.

THE NATIONAL MEMORIAL FOR PEACE & JUSTICE

Lynching emerged as a vicious tool of racial control in the South after the Civil War. Lynchings were violent and public events designed to reestablish White supremacy by terrorizing Black people and suppressing their civil rights. Many African Americans were tortured to death in front of picnicking spectators for things like wearing their military uniforms, bumping into a White person, or not using the appropriate title when addressing a White person. The Equal Justice Initiative (EJI) – a nonprofit organization established in 1989 to end mass incarceration and excessive punishment and challenge racial and economic injustice – has documented nearly 6,500 racial terror lynchings that occurred in the U.S. between 1865 and 1950. The architecturally significant six-acre National Memorial for Peace and Justice lists the names of lynching victims on over 800 suspended Corten steel columns, one for each county where a racial terror lynching took place. The Legacy Museum: From Enslavement to Mass Incarceration uses compelling visuals and data-rich exhibits to educate the nation about the legacy of slavery, racial terrorism, the Jim Crow South and the world's largest prison system. More than 750,000 people visited EJI's sites in the first 20 months of their opening in 2018.

CIVIL RIGHTS MEMORIAL

The Civil Rights Memorial, designed by sculptor Maya Y. Lin for the Southern Poverty Law Center (SPLC), honors 41 victims whose lives were taken by racists during the Civil Rights Movement between 1954 and 1968. Water flows down the curved backdrop of black granite engraved with Dr. King's well-known paraphrase of Amos 5:24 – "...until justice rolls down like waters and righteousness like a mighty stream." Water also flows across the stone table bearing names of the martyrs, and visitors are encouraged to touch the names and reflect on their sacrifices. SPLC co-founder Morris Dees commissioned Lin, who is best known for creating the Vietnam Veterans Memorial in Washington, D.C.

FREEDOM RIDES MUSEUM

The arrest of Howard University law student Bruce Boynton for refusing to leave a "Whites only" Trailways bus station café in Richmond in 1958 resulted in the U.S. Supreme Court's 1960 *Boynton v. Virginia* decision that cited the Equal Protection Clause of the 14th Amendment and desegregated interstate transportation facilities.

The Freedom Riders set out to test compliance with the *Boynton* decision at bus stations across the South in a campaign that began May 4, 1961, when 13 members of the interracial Congress of Racial Equality left Washington, D.C., in Greyhound and Trailways buses bound for New Orleans. Over the summer, more than 400 Black and White students participated in 60 bus trips.

Trouble found them in Rock Hill, South Carolina, where Klansmen beat John Lewis and Al Bigelow when they tried to sit in a "Whites only" waiting room. On Mother's Day, May 14, segregationists outside Anniston, Alabama, firebombed a Greyhound bus with panicked Freedom Riders aboard. Locals saw the students as "outside agitators" challenging Southern racial customs. Sites in Anniston related to the event were designated the Freedom Riders National Monument in 2017 by President Barack Obama, and the National Park Service is now developing them as memorials.

A week later, on May 20, when Nashville Freedom Riders including James Zwerg and again John Lewis arrived at the Greyhound station in Montgomery, a White mob of 300 segregationists struck the integrationists with chains and clubs. When the college students gathered the next night at First Baptist, the violent crowd of White supremacists had grown to 3,000 and surrounded the Ripley Street sanctuary, threatening to burn alive those trapped inside. Notified of the danger by Dr. King, Attorney General Robert Kennedy convinced Gov. John Patterson to declare martial law, using the National Guard to protect the civil rights activists. The Greyhound bus station at 210 South Court Street is now the Freedom Rides Museum, where the Alabama Historical Commission hosted campaign veterans at a 60th anniversary reunion in 2021.

ROSA PARKS MUSEUM

The famous bus ride of Rosa Parks from the corner of Dexter Avenue lasted only a couple of blocks. A life-size statue of the seamstress marks the spot where she boarded the bus after work on Thursday, Dec. 1, 1955. Two stops later in front of the Empire Theater, she refused to yield her seat to a White man when told to do so. On the 45th anniversary of her arrest, Troy University opened the Rosa Parks Museum and Library constructed on this corner at 252 Montgomery Street, with exhibits created by the legendary design firm Ralph Applebaum Associates. Among the exhibits is a diorama depicting Dr. King's kitchen table epiphany when he feared the Montgomery Bus Boycott would fail. "It seemed at that moment I could hear an inner voice saying to me, 'Martin Luther, stand up for righteousness. Stand up for truth,'" Dr. King said. "My uncertainty disappeared. I was ready to face anything."

1957

LITTLE ROCK
ARKANSAS

The year after the U.S. Supreme Court ruled that school segregation was unconstitutional, the court reiterated its ruling, calling on school districts to desegregate their public schools "with all deliberate speed." Unlike many districts that developed strategies to resist public school desegregation, school officials in Little Rock, Arkansas, agreed to comply, and established rigorous interviews to find Black students they deemed most suitable for admission to White schools.

Central High School, Little Rock's largest, interviewed 80 and selected nine based on grades and attendance: Melba Patillo, Elizabeth Eckford, Ernest Green, Gloria Ray, Carlotta Walls, Terrence Roberts, Jefferson Thomas, Minnijean Brown and Thelma Mothershed. Black newspaper editor and political activist Daisy Lee Bates, who had become president of the state chapter of the NAACP in 1952, opened her home as their headquarters and became their organizer.

On Sept. 4, 1957, Gov. Orval Faubus deployed the National Guard to "preserve the peace" by blocking the Little Rock Nine from admission. When Black students again tried to attend school on Sept. 23, a mob of taunting White supremacists prevented their entry. President Dwight Eisenhower responded to the Little Rock Crisis by dispatching nearly 1,000 paratroopers from the 101st Airborne Division from Fort Campbell, Kentucky, and federalized 10,000 National Guard troops to ensure that the Black students could attend White schools.

Two days later, the students were admitted for classes. Despite the presence of Army units on campus, the nine were subjected to petty harassment by their White classmates for the rest of the academic year.

Daisy Bates ignored the numerous threats over her activism. But White business owners withheld advertising from the weekly newspaper she and her husband owned, resulting in low revenue and causing it to close in 1959. Three years later, she published her account of the school integration battle, *The Long Shadow of Little Rock*. Bates became the only woman to address the 1963 March on Washington, substituting for Myrlie Evers, the

Daisy Bates

Elizabeth Eckford was one of nine students who integrated Little Rock Central High School and endured persistent harassment by White students and local residents.

widow of martyred Mississippi activist Medgar Evers. In Bates' "Tribute to Negro Women Fighters for Freedom," she said that "all the women pledge that we will join hands with you. We will kneel-in, we will sit-in, until we can eat in any corner in the United States. We will walk until we are free, until we can walk to any school and take our children to any school in the United States. And we will sit-in and we will kneel-in and we will lie-in if necessary until every Negro in America can vote. This we pledge to the women of America."

The integration of the Arkansas school came a year after a Tennessee federal judge ordered the admission of Black students in a White school in Clinton, Tennessee. Enrolled on Aug. 26, 1956, the Clinton 12 entered a high school surrounded by racial strife. Tensions persisted and on Oct. 5, 1958, a bomb destroyed much of the school. A fundraising campaign by North Carolina evangelist Billy Graham raised money to rebuild the now desegregated school, which marked another victory in the decades-long effort to desegregate education in the U.S. No incidents were reported after the school was rebuilt.

In 1999, Arkansas native President Bill Clinton honored the Little Rock Nine when he presented each with a Congressional Gold Medal, the highest civilian award bestowed by Congress, given to those who have provided outstanding service to the country.

The Little Rock Nine entered Central High School escorted by armed federal troops.

LITTLE ROCK CENTRAL HIGH SCHOOL NATIONAL HISTORIC SITE

The high school students known as the Little Rock Nine became symbols of courage and optimism during desegregation. Their story comes alive at the visitor center and museum, which offers ranger-led tours of the still-functioning school.

President Dwight D. Eisenhower sent troops to provide order and protection for Little Rock Central High School's first Black students.

Now designated as the Little Rock Central High School National Historic Site, the school is still in operation today.

DAISY BATES HOUSE

Arkansas civil rights activist Daisy Bates opened her home at 1207 West 28th Street as a command post for the Little Rock Nine who integrated Central High School in 1957. The U.S. Department of the Interior listed the Bates residence as a National Historic Landmark in 2001. The state legislature voted in 2019 to place statues of Bates and singer Johnny Cash in the U.S. Capitol's Statuary Hall to represent Arkansas.

LITTLE ROCK NINE MEMORIAL AT THE STATE CAPITOL

The Little Rock Nine Memorial honors the courage of the African American students who enrolled at Little Rock Central High School and began the process of desegregating secondary education in 1957. Located on the grounds of the Arkansas Capitol, the memorial features bronze sculptures of the nine, along with plaques bearing quotations from each of them.

1960

GREENSBORO
NORTH CAROLINA

Franklin McCain fully expected to be arrested and put in jail when he and three other Black college students sat down to integrate the Greensboro Woolworth's lunch counter on Monday, Feb. 1, 1960. Despite being dressed in his ROTC uniform, McCain assumed that store manager Curly Harris would swear out warrants against the four for trespassing. When they politely ordered coffee and doughnuts, they were simply ignored. So McCain, Ezell Blair Jr., Joseph McNeil and David Richmond, all from North Carolina Agricultural & Technical State University, sat quietly at the counter until Harris closed the store early. They left, telling the manager they would return the next day. On Tuesday, 19 more students, including women from Bennett College, another historically Black college, sat at the same counter. On Wednesday, 85 joined them and filled the store's 65 seats. By Saturday, some 900 students protested the exclusion of service to Black people at the Woolworth and nearby Kress variety stores. This first sit-in at Woolworth by the Greensboro Four inspired a larger nonviolent sit-in movement that swept across the South and the nation, eventually leading to the end of "Whites only" lunch counters and segregation in public accommodations. On May 10, 1960, the segregated lunch counters in Nashville became the first in a Southern city to accept Black and White customers equally.

Blair and a number of other students had heard Dr. Martin Luther King Jr. speak at Bennett College two years earlier and debated what they could do to advance civil rights. They developed plans in consultation with the Bennett Belles, as the school's students were called, who served as lookouts at the first sit-in. The sit-ins in Greensboro lasted six months. Prior to the attempt to desegregate Woolworth's lunch counter, the Greensboro store had served more meals per day than any Woolworth in the South and ranked 54th in sales among the 3,000 locations across the nation. The company brass in New York told the manager it was up to him to decide whether to serve Black customers or not. When manager Harris finally integrated on July 25, he insisted that his own employees would be the first Black patrons

Sign from Woolworth's lunch counter

Students staged a sit-in to protest Woolworth's "Whites only" lunch counter.

served at his Woolworth lunch counter. Later that spring, the Greensboro Four and the Bennett Belles joined other sit-in veterans from across the South in organizing the Student Nonviolent Coordinating Committee at a meeting held at Shaw University in nearby Raleigh.

Business at the Greensboro Woolworth initially increased after desegregation, to the point that the lunch counter had to be expanded. In 1990, on the 30th anniversary of the first sit-in, the Greensboro Four returned to the store to recall that fateful day when they launched the student movement. But the store closed in 1994. Memorialists restored the Greensboro Woolworth to house the International Civil Rights Center & Museum, which opened Feb. 1, 2010, the 50th anniversary of the first sit-in.

On Oct. 11, 2016, President Barack Obama became the first sitting president to visit NC A&T, coming to campus to tape an ESPN event.

The significance of the Greensboro Four was further acknowledged with the launch of the U.S. Civil Rights Trail in 2018 and its full-page ad in *Time* magazine's Jan. 29 issue. The ad featured spliced period and current photos of the lunch counter with the headline "See where they took a seat to make a stand." The Woolworth site is one of dozens of inspiring landmarks on the U.S. Civil Rights Trail. Lunch counter stools from the Greensboro Woolworth are on display at the Smithsonian's National Museum of African American History and Culture in Washington, D.C. They are featured in the exhibit "Defending Freedom, Defining Freedom: The Era of Segregation."

The Greensboro sit-ins gained national attention and sparked protests at other Woolworth locations, such as Harlem in New York City.

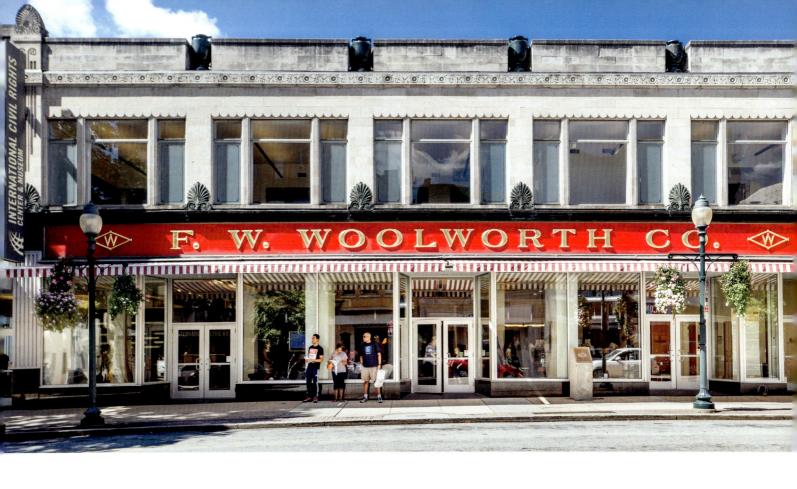

INTERNATIONAL CIVIL RIGHTS CENTER & MUSEUM (WOOLWORTH)

The museum's mission is to commemorate the Greensboro Four and their role in launching the sit-in movement that inspired peaceful direct-action demonstrations across the country. The seats and counter remain in the building in their original footprint. The museum includes exhibits and videos about the Greensboro Four and the greater American Civil Rights Movement. Guided tours are available.

The nonviolent sit-ins at F.W. Woolworth Co. in Greensboro were the first in a movement that spread across the South.

Today, the Greensboro Woolworth is home to the International Civil Rights Center & Museum, which continues to tell the story of the Greensboro Four.

"Let us, if it's necessary, be the victims of violence but never the perpetrators of violence. And then we will be able to stand before our brothers in the South and say, 'We will match your capacity to inflict suffering by our capacity to endure suffering ... Burn our homes, and we'll still love you ... Take our children and spit in their faces ... and we will still love you ...' We will wear you down by our capacity to suffer ... We will so appeal to your heart and conscience that we will win you in the process."

MARTIN LUTHER KING JR.
from his speech "Room in the Inn" delivered to Bennett College in Greensboro on Feb. 1, 1958, two years before the sit-in at Woolworth

FEBRUARY ONE MONUMENT

On Feb. 1, 1960, North Carolina A&T University students David Richmond, Franklin McCain, Ezell Blair Jr. (Jibreel Khazan) and Joseph McNeil carried out the famous lunch counter sit-in at the F.W. Woolworth store. An outdoor statue of the four brave men marks their place in the nation's civil rights history.

1960

NASHVILLE
TENNESSEE

On April 19, 1960, Diane Nash, leader of the Nashville Student Movement, silently led 3,000 students the three miles from Tennessee Agricultural & Industrial State University to the Davidson County Courthouse for a confrontation with the mayor. She was flanked by activists Bernard Lafayette and the Rev. C.T. Vivian. Nash, a Fisk University co-ed, and her fellow marchers were angry over a pre-dawn bombing that had shattered the home of NAACP attorney Z. Alexander Looby. He and his wife, Grafta, escaped with their lives. A prominent Black member of the City Council, Looby handled the legal cases that arose from 10 weeks of peaceful Nashville sit-ins to oppose segregation of city lunch counters.

The Rev. James Lawson, who taught workshops in nonviolent activism, had led the first mass meeting of the student movement Feb. 12 at First Baptist Church at Eighth Avenue North and Charlotte Pike. The next day, more than 100 trained activists walked through the historic Arcade Mall and reached the targeted lunch counters on Fifth Avenue. Over the course of the Nashville campaign, sit-ins were staged at numerous stores in the central business district. Participants, primarily Black college students, were often verbally or physically attacked by White onlookers. Despite their refusal to retaliate, more than 150 students were arrested for refusing to vacate store lunch counters when ordered to do so by the police.

On the day of the march to the courthouse, Mayor Ben West was outside waiting for the group. After a brief, heated exchange between West and Vivian, Nash quietly posed the question that would change history: "Mayor," she asked, "do you recommend that the lunch counters be desegregated?"

To the surprise of many, West answered, "Yes."

Three weeks later, on May 10, under a secret agreement between government and business leaders, Nashville made history. Black customers ate at Fifth Avenue lunch counters where sit-ins had previously been waged, and the Music City quietly became the first city in the South to desegregate.

Many of the leaders of Nashville's

John Lewis

Ten weeks of sit-ins by students, including John Hardy (left) and Curtis Murphy, led to Nashville being the first city in the South to desegregate lunch counters.

movement went on to lead other fights. The next year, Nash, Vivian, Lafayette and his roommate, John Lewis, participated in the more dangerous Freedom Rides that were met with violence in South Carolina, Alabama and Mississippi. The Civil Rights Movement marked another advance when the Interstate Commerce Commission, responding to the integrationists and recognizing the *Boynton* ruling of the year before, required an end to segregated bus terminals and travel effective Nov. 1, 1961.

Knowing they might die, the civil rights activists recalled questions Lewis had raised early in their sit-in training Feb. 12: "If not us, then who? If not now, then when?" The quote is prominently displayed in the Civil Rights Room at the Nashville Public Library.

Upon returning to Nashville years later, now U.S. Congressman John Lewis recalled the sit-ins. "The first time I got arrested in this city, I felt free," he said. "I have not looked back since."

Civil rights veterans Lewis and Vivian died a few hours apart on July 17, 2020.

Today, *Witness Walls*, a memorial by artist Walter Hood, stands at Nashville's Public Square Park at the historic courthouse, near where Diane Nash and fellow students silently demanded racial equality. Standing more than seven feet tall, the sculpture places visitors among the heroic people who took part in the 1960 demonstrations. The walls use shadow and light to capture the metaphor of struggle as figures and scenes emerge and retreat along the coarse surface.

Pin promoting the first Freedom Ride, which the Congress of Racial Equality (CORE) sponsored in 1961

C.T. Vivian (left), Diane Nash and Bernard Lafayette (right) led the march on City Hall.

DAVIDSON COUNTY COURTHOUSE & *WITNESS WALLS*

In April 1960, after months of sit-in demonstrations, economic boycotts and Freedom Rides, a crowd of over 3,000 descended on the Davidson County Courthouse to protest segregation. Today, visitors can experience *Witness Walls*, an art installation that memorializes the brave men and women across Nashville who took action against inequality.

GRIGGS HALL AT AMERICAN BAPTIST COLLEGE

Built in 1923, Griggs Hall was the first building to be erected on the campus of American Baptist College, which opened in 1924. The school educated many participants of the Nashville sit-in movement.

FIFTH AVENUE HISTORIC DISTRICT

This location was the site of a number of successful sit-ins that served as models for later demonstrations in the South. Located at 221 Fifth Avenue North, the Woolworth building is a registered historic site as part of the Fifth Avenue Historic District in downtown Nashville.

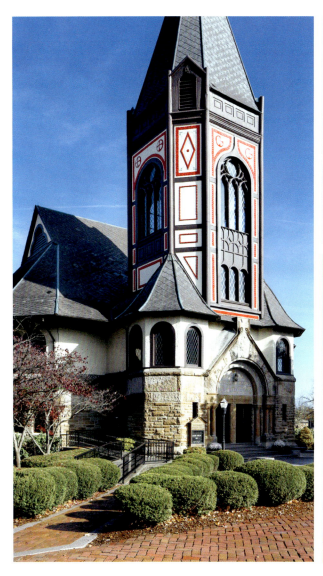

FISK UNIVERSITY

Fisk University, founded in 1866, was the first African American institution to receive accreditation from the Southern Association of Colleges and Schools. Many of the university's students were the backbone of sit-in demonstrations that successfully desegregated Nashville's lunch counters.

1960

NEW ORLEANS
LOUISIANA

On June 7, 1892, Homer Plessy, an African American New Orleans railroad passenger, was arrested at the Press Street Railroad Yards. Because of his light complexion, he was able to purchase a ticket for the "Whites only" car with the intention of challenging Louisiana's 1890 "separate railway carriage" law. Authorities arrested Plessy who, after confirming his race when questioned, refused to change cars. Convicted, Plessy filed suit against the presiding judge, John H. Ferguson, arguing that the law violated the Equal Protection Clause of the 14th Amendment. On May 18, 1896, the U.S. Supreme Court delivered its 8-1 racist landmark decision in *Plessy v. Ferguson* that denied segregated railroad cars for Black citizens were necessarily inferior. The result enshrined the doctrine of "separate but equal" as a constitutional justification for racial segregation for the next half-century. In 2009, descendants of Plessy and Ferguson erected historic markers at the rail yard and St. Louis Cemetery No. 1, the oldest in the city, where Plessy is buried. Memorialists gather at the rail yard on June 7 to commemorate the anniversary of Plessy's significant act of civil disobedience.

Black parents in Kansas who wanted their children to attend White schools closer to their homes challenged the "separate but equal" ruling in 1950. As a result of the *Brown v. Board of Education of Topeka* decision in 1954 that overturned *Plessy v. Ferguson*, 6-year-old Ruby Bridges of New Orleans became famous among the South's first Black pupils to integrate an all-White school when she began attending William Frantz Elementary on Nov. 14, 1960. That day, scores of angry White parents jeered as four federal officers escorted her to and from kindergarten, an event immortalized in the Norman Rockwell painting *The Problem We All Live With*. During Ruby's first year, she struggled emotionally, as she and her teacher sat alone in a classroom boycotted by White students. Similarly across town in the Ninth Ward, U.S. marshals escorted Black first-graders Leona Tate, Tessie Prevost and Gail Etienne past harassing White parents and into McDonogh 19. For months, the girls, called the "McDonogh Three," attended the formerly all-White school as its only students, holding recess inside as a safety precaution.

Like college students in Greensboro, Nashville and other Southern cities, Black youths in New Orleans staged sit-ins at "Whites only" lunch

Ruby Bridges

Federal officers escorted 6-year-old Ruby Bridges, one of the first Black students to integrate New Orleans public schools, to and from class at William Frantz Elementary.

counters in 1960. On Canal Street, they challenged segregation at Woolworth and McCrory's, with both stores eventually relenting and integrating. The more sophisticated dining establishments in the city had long drawn visitors. At the height of the movement, Chef Leah Chase welcomed civil rights activists such as Thurgood Marshall, Black entertainers and major professional sports stars to Dooky Chase's in the Tremé neighborhood where she fed them feasts of outstanding Creole comfort food. The cultural and culinary legend received a James Beard Lifetime Achievement Award in 2016 before her death at age 96 in 2019.

One of Louisiana's pioneers for racial justice was the Rev. T.J. Jemison, pastor of Mount Zion First Baptist Church in Baton Rouge. In 1953, he led the Black community in the nation's first postwar boycott for better seating on city buses. For eight days, Black citizens organized a free carpool pickup system at the Old State Capitol and Memorial Stadium until the city settled. Two years later, Jemison advised Dr. Martin Luther King Jr. on setting up ride-sharing for the better known Montgomery Bus Boycott. On Feb. 14, 1957, at the formal incorporation of the Southern Christian Leadership Conference at the New Zion Baptist Church in New Orleans, the members elected Jemison secretary. He served eight months before being replaced by the Rev. Fred L. Shuttlesworth.

Ku Klux Klan violence greeted the nonviolent movement led by A.Z. Young and Robert Hicks when activists tested compliance with the Civil Rights Act in the Louisiana lumber town of Bogalusa in February 1965. Faced with an absence of police protection from White supremacists, Young and Hicks founded Deacons for Defense and Justice, an African American group that embraced armed resistance. For two years, the struggle raged on, culminating in the August 1967 march from Bogalusa to Baton Rouge, a nine-day, 106-mile trek to raise international awareness of ongoing Klan violence and resistance to desegregation. By the time the marchers – now protected by National Guardsmen – reached the Capitol, their number had grown to 600 Black people.

The Problem We All Live With by Norman Rockwell depicts the bravery of kindergartner Ruby Bridges in the face of racial hatred.

WILLIAM FRANTZ ELEMENTARY SCHOOL

Six-year-old Ruby Bridges became the first Black student to attend the previously all-White school. While the former William Frantz Elementary building now houses a charter school, Akili Academy, Ruby's legacy is preserved at the site with a statue in the courtyard along with the restored Classroom 2306, which looks as it did when she attended the school.

1963

BIRMINGHAM
ALABAMA

A stunned world watched Birmingham's White policemen sic dogs on nonviolent Black protestors who were challenging the city's strict segregation laws during the 1963 Spring Demonstrations in Kelly Ingram Park. The civil rights campaign included an economic boycott of downtown stores where Black customers could not use the "Whites only" dressing rooms, elevators, toilets, water fountains or lunch counters. The demonstrations marked the culmination of eight years of local protests led by the Rev. Fred L. Shuttlesworth, who members of the Ku Klux Klan had beaten and tried to kill by bombing his Bethel Baptist Church three times. As Southern Christian Leadership Conference secretary, Shuttlesworth invited the organization's president, Dr. Martin Luther King Jr., and vice president, the Rev. Ralph David Abernathy, to bring the group's resources to Birmingham. On Good Friday, the three men led a march and then suffered arrest by police. In response to the city's White pastors calling the protests "untimely," an incarcerated Dr. King echoed St. Paul in his "Letter from Birmingham Jail" to morally justify the movement, arguing famously that "injustice anywhere is a threat to justice everywhere."

As a recalcitrant city government led by Eugene "Bull" Connor defended White supremacy, the April weeks saw more arrests of Black adults, depleting the movement's number of volunteers. Thinking his suppression had worked, an astonished Connor watched the "Children's Crusade" unfold as hundreds of Black students – recruited by activists from local schools – marched down the stairs of 16th Street Baptist Church and into Kelly Ingram Park. Unable to arrest the thousands of African Americans who joined the campaign in early May, Connor grew violent, ordering firemen to train high-powered water hoses on the Black youths, knocking them down. On May 7, Black protesters outmaneuvered police, filling the White business and shopping districts as civil order collapsed.

Alarmed at international condemnation, President John F. Kennedy intervened, announcing on May 10 a truce between movement leaders and White businessmen. Realizing Connor had failed to uphold segregation, Klansmen tried to assassinate Dr. King by bombing the A.G. Gaston Motel and the home of Dr. King's brother,

Mug shot of Dr. Martin Luther King Jr.

The image of teenager Walter Gadsden being attacked by a police dog in Birmingham brought national outrage.

A.D. King. On June 11, Kennedy responded to Gov. George Wallace's stand against desegregating the University of Alabama — but more importantly the racial tension that had spread beyond Birmingham across the nation — by delivering one of the most impassioned speeches on civil rights ever given by a president. Kennedy called White supremacy immoral and promised Congress comprehensive legislation, saying, "The heart of the question is whether all Americans are to be afforded equal rights and equal opportunities."

As the federal courts ordered school desegregation in Alabama, Gov. Wallace fomented racial hatred. The day before integration occurred, Black girls gathered in the basement of 16th Street Baptist Church for Youth Sunday, Sept. 15, 1963. Dynamite hidden by Klansmen beside the wall exploded with a roar. The blast killed Addie Mae Collins, Denise McNair, Carole Robertson and Cynthia Wesley. FBI Director J. Edgar Hoover, who harassed Dr. King with wiretaps, thwarted a timely prosecution of suspects by sealing federal evidence. In 1977, Alabama Attorney General Bill Baxley earned a conviction of one of the suspects, and in 2001 U.S. Attorney Doug Jones retried the cold case and convicted two other Klansmen.

The Birmingham demonstrations signaled the climax of the Civil Rights Movement, and the subsequent Civil Rights Act of 1964 indicated a watershed in national race relations. The landmark act outlawed discrimination based on race, color, religion, sex, national origin and, in time, disability and sexual orientation. It prohibited discrimination in public accommodations and federally assisted programs, promoted voting rights and school desegregation, and proposed equal employment opportunities.

One of America's most powerful museums, the Birmingham Civil Rights Institute, opened adjacent to Kelly Ingram Park in 1992. Next door, 16th Street Baptist Church offers an emotional tour about the four martyred girls, featuring personal items and a clock stopped at 10:22, the time of the blast. In 2013, President Barack Obama presented Congressional Gold Medals to the families of the murdered youths. In 2017, he created the Birmingham Civil Rights National Monument, a National Park Service unit, that encompasses the museum, motel, park and both 16th Street Baptist and Bethel Baptist churches.

Clock from 16th Street Baptist Church

City authorities targeted student demonstrators with blasts from a high-pressure fire hose to break up the protest at Kelly Ingram Park.

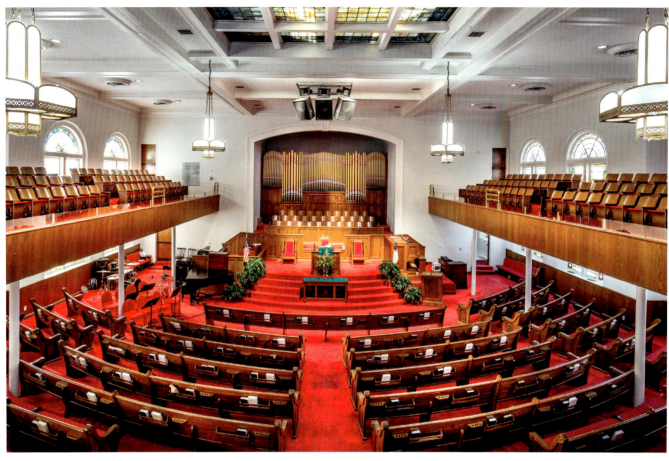

16TH STREET BAPTIST CHURCH

The brick church and adjacent parsonage that noted Black architect Wallace Rayfield designed are the most iconic structures in the Birmingham Civil Rights National Monument. After the Ku Klux Klan bombed the church and killed four Black girls in 1963, the children of Wales in the United Kingdom collected coins for a memorial stained-glass window. Artist John Petts depicted a Black man pushing away hatred and injustice with his right hand while offering his left hand in forgiveness. Sixteenth Street Baptist Church is on the U.S. Tentative List for UNESCO World Heritage.

Sixteenth Street Baptist Church is still active in the community despite its tragic past and welcomes visitors to tour its historic building.

A sanctuary for civil rights activism and planning, 16th Street Baptist Church was bombed by members of the Ku Klux Klan in 1963, killing four young girls.

KELLY INGRAM PARK

The four-acre park that fronts the 16th Street Baptist Church served as a central staging ground for large-scale demonstrations against segregation in May 1963. The Rev. Fred Shuttlesworth and Dr. Martin Luther King Jr. demanded equal access for Black citizens to department store jobs, lunch counters, water fountains, restrooms and dressing rooms. Birmingham police and fire departments responded by attacking youthful demonstrators with police dogs and powerful fire hoses, tactics that shocked America. Now, monuments and statues interpret the events of the Spring Demonstrations. Originally for Whites only and renamed in 1932 to honor local firefighter Kelly Ingram, the first sailor in the U.S. Navy to be killed in World War I, the park was rezoned "colored" by the city during the 1950s.

BETHEL BAPTIST CHURCH

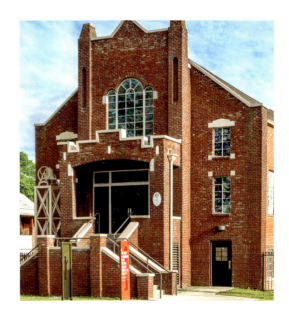

From 1953 to 1961, Bethel was the home church of the Rev. Fred L. Shuttlesworth who braved beatings, bombings and fire hoses to push Birmingham to the forefront of the Civil Rights Movement. Shuttlesworth joined Dr. King to establish the Southern Christian Leadership Conference in 1957 to coordinate local protest groups in the South. In 1962, Shuttlesworth invited Dr. King to Birmingham to provide "star power" for the Easter shopping boycott as part of the 1963 Spring Demonstrations that generated hundreds of arrests. After the Bethel Baptist congregation moved into a new sanctuary in 1997, it made the Historic Bethel Baptist Church at 3233 28th Avenue North into a museum that is now part of the Birmingham Civil Rights National Monument. When the former pastor and civil rights activist died in 2008, the city honored him with burial in the historic Oak Hill Cemetery north of the Birmingham-Jefferson Convention Complex and by renaming the airport the Birmingham-Shuttlesworth International Airport.

BIRMINGHAM CIVIL RIGHTS INSTITUTE

Housed in a building designed by African American architect J. Max Bond Jr., this modern museum features a rendition of a segregated Birmingham in the 1950s, a replica of a burned Freedom Riders bus and the actual door to the jail cell that held Dr. King. The institute is home to an expansive archive of documents from the Civil Rights Movement and nearly 500 recorded oral histories relevant to the period.

 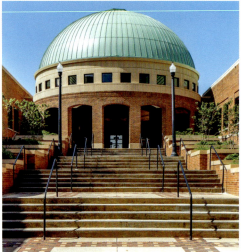 

"Injustice anywhere is a threat to justice everywhere. We are caught in an inescapable network of mutuality, tied in a single garment of destiny. Whatever affects one directly affects all indirectly … We know through painful experience that freedom is never voluntarily given by the oppressor; it must be demanded by the oppressed."

MARTIN LUTHER KING JR.
from "Letter from Birmingham Jail," written April 1963

1963

JACKSON
MISSISSIPPI

In the eight years that civil rights activist Medgar Evers served as the first NAACP field secretary in Mississippi, he led dangerous voter registration drives, investigated nine racially motivated murders and examined widespread crimes aimed at intimidating Black citizens. Because of Evers' work, the governor ordered law enforcement officers in the Mississippi State Sovereignty Commission to spy on him, as did the Ku Klux Klan, which tried to kill him. On June 12, 1963, the 37-year-old veteran, husband and father of three arrived at his Jackson home after midnight and parked behind his wife's Chevrolet under the carport. As he stepped out of his Oldsmobile carrying a stack of "Jim Crow Must Go" T-shirts, sniper Byron De La Beckwith fired a fatal shot from 150 feet away that struck Evers in the back and spiraled on to pierce the exterior wall and lodge by the refrigerator. The assassin dropped the military .30-06 Enfield rifle bearing fingerprints and fled. Evers struggled toward the house and died an hour later.

Tried twice for the murder and despite overwhelming evidence showing his guilt, Beckwith was acquitted by a pair of all-White juries. Decades later, renewed interest in the cold case led investigative reporter Jerry Mitchell of Jackson's *Clarion-Ledger* to discover additional evidence against Beckwith in the death of Evers. Thirty years after the crime, a racially mixed jury convicted Beckwith of murder. He died in prison in 2001 at age 80. Widow Myrlie Evers donated the house to Tougaloo College, which opened it as a museum. Listed on the Mississippi Freedom Trail, the National Historic Landmark became the Medgar and Myrlie Evers Home National Monument in 2019. The bullet hole can still be seen in the kitchen wall.

A film of Evers' life and the Enfield rifle that caused his death are showcased in the awe-inspiring Mississippi Civil Rights Museum that opened during the state's bicentennial in 2017. The museum galleries encircle a central space called "This Little Light of Mine" where music of the Civil Rights Movement swells and light glows brighter as more

Medgar Evers

The assassination of Medgar Evers in the driveway of his home ended his tireless work for voting rights and his investigation of crimes against Black citizens.

visitors gather near. Other documentary films incorporated into the exhibits explain how the U.S. Supreme Court's 1954 *Brown v. Board of Education* desegregation decision and Emmett Till's brutal murder the following year fueled the movement. Mug shots of civil rights activists, including college students arrested as Freedom Riders in 1961, paper the walls. A grim series of monoliths are engraved with names of lynching victims by year.

Another documentary recounts the murders of college students James Chaney, who was a Black youth from Meridian, Mississippi, and Michael Schwerner and Andrew Goodman, both White New Yorkers. They had answered the call of the Student Nonviolent Coordinating Committee, which had recruited Northern and White students to register Black voters during Mississippi Freedom Summer in 1964. Two months after the three disappeared, a tipster informed the FBI of an earthen dam containing their buried bodies. A 1967 federal trial convicted seven but acquitted nine of the White conspirators identified with the crime. Years later, reporter Jerry Mitchell assembled evidence used to convict Klansman Edgar Ray Killen with manslaughter for recruiting the mob that carried out the murders. In 2018, Killen died at age 92 in the Mississippi State Penitentiary at Parchman Farm, the same prison that had housed the arrested Freedom Riders upon their arrival in Jackson in 1961.

Pin promoting voter registration drives sponsored by the Student Nonviolent Coordinating Committee (SNCC)

The FBI issued a missing persons flier when civil rights volunteers Andrew Goodman, James Chaney and Michael Schwerner disappeared.

MISSISSIPPI CIVIL RIGHTS MUSEUM

Eight galleries examine the state's African American history, beginning with slavery, emancipation, community building and Black leadership during and after Reconstruction. The exhibits continue, exploring disfranchisement, segregation, the White supremacist "Closed Society" of Mississippi, Black resistance during the civil rights struggle and Black political empowerment, leading to the resulting modern Mississippi. Exhibits and artifacts emphasize the essential role played by the Black family and Black church. A re-created jail cell and tear gas canisters represent James Meredith's integration of Ole Miss. Immersive theaters spotlight the lives and deaths of Emmett Till and Medgar Evers. Other exhibits highlight the volunteers of the Freedom Rides, the Freedom Summer campaign to register Black voters, and Fannie Lou Hamer and the Mississippi Freedom Democratic Party.

MEDGAR & MYRLIE EVERS HOME MUSEUM

When house hunting in 1956, Medgar Evers liked that the fashionable ranch-style structure at 2332 Margaret Walker Alexander Drive had no front door. The Mississippi NAACP field secretary hoped the side carport entrance and location in Jackson's new Black middle-class neighborhood would provide more security. Tragically, that did not prevent his assassination on June 12, 1963. Known today as the Medgar and Myrlie Evers Home National Monument, the historic house museum served as a location for the 1996 filming of *Ghosts of Mississippi*, which tells Evers' story and includes cameo performances by his widow and children. On the 50th anniversary of his death, Evers' alma mater Alcorn State University unveiled a statue of him on its campus in Lorman.

1963

WASHINGTON
DISTRICT OF COLUMBIA

The nation's capital is filled with uplifting monuments and outstanding architecture that represent ideals of freedom and democracy. To many citizens, the U.S. Supreme Court Building symbolizes landmark rulings such as the *Brown v. Board of Education of Topeka* decision that abolished legal race-based segregation. In the red-curtained first-floor courtroom, NAACP lead attorney Thurgood Marshall argued before the nine White justices that separate schools violated the Equal Protection Clause of the 14th Amendment. Newly appointed Chief Justice Earl Warren crafted a unanimous decision released on May 17, 1954, that agreed with Marshall and declared as unconstitutional and a lie the previous "separate but equal" standard.

Near the Supreme Court Building is the East Portico of the U.S. Capitol where in 2013 President Barack Obama proclaimed in his second inaugural address, "We, the people, declare today that the most evident of truths – that all of us are created equal – is the star that guides us still; just as it guided our forebears through Seneca Falls, and Selma, and Stonewall; just as it guided all those men and women, sung and unsung, who left footprints along this great Mall, to hear a preacher say that we cannot walk alone; to hear a King proclaim that our individual freedom is inextricably bound to the freedom of every soul on Earth."

It was at the Lincoln Memorial that Dr. Martin Luther King Jr. gave his "I Have a Dream" speech on Aug. 28, 1963, during the March on Washington for Jobs and Freedom. Surprisingly, the phrase "I have a dream" appeared nowhere in his prepared text, which – with the help of Black attorney Clarence Jones – Dr. King had modeled on the Gettysburg Address, calling on White leaders to live up to the ideals of the Declaration of Independence and U.S. Constitution. Twelve minutes into his oration, the great gospel singer Mahalia Jackson, who had performed earlier, sensed a growing listlessness in the crowd and, remembering a refrain from a speech Dr. King had given in Detroit, called out, "Tell them about the dream, Martin. Tell them about the dream." She had heard him in Detroit on June 23 tell a massive crowd in Cobo Hall, "I have a dream that one day, right down in Georgia and Mississippi and Alabama, the sons of former slaves and the

Pin worn by participants in
the March on Washington

Against the backdrop of the Lincoln Memorial, Dr. Martin Luther King Jr. addressed the crowd gathered for the March on Washington for Jobs and Freedom.

sons of former slave owners will be able to live together as brothers. I have a dream this afternoon that one day, one day little White children and little Negro children will be able to join hands as brothers and sisters."

That afternoon in Washington, Dr. King slid his script to the side of the lectern and seamlessly began to reprise his Detroit speech. Jones, who was on the dais, turned to a compatriot and said, "The people don't know it, but they're about to go to church." The last five minutes were extemporaneous, magical and mesmerizing. Today, a marker commemorating the moment rests where Dr. King delivered his powerful words.

Elsewhere on the National Mall stands the only statue to a non-president. The Martin Luther King Jr. Memorial, commissioned by Dr. King's college fraternity Alpha Phi Alpha, is set along the Tidal Basin, visually connecting the Jefferson and Lincoln memorials. A sentence from Dr. King's speech inspired the "Stone of Hope," the 30-foot sculpture that seemingly emerges from the granite, leaving behind the "Mountain of Despair."

The nation's capital is also where Vice President Kamala Harris began college life in 1982 at Howard University. She lived in Eton Towers dormitory on Vermont Avenue Northwest and pledged Alpha Kappa Alpha, the nation's oldest Black sorority. After attending Howard, often referred to as "the Black Harvard," she rose to statewide office in California before becoming a U.S. senator and, in 2021, President Joe Biden's vice president. Just as Obama was the first African American man to occupy the White House, Harris is the first woman – Black or White – elected to national office.

The contributions and struggles of Black people over four centuries are displayed at the National Museum of African American History and Culture located near the Washington Monument. The collection of more than 36,000 artifacts helps trace the Black experience through enslavement, the Civil War, Reconstruction, segregation and civil rights to today. U.S. Rep. John Lewis of Georgia labored for 28 years to secure funding. He celebrated the museum's opening in 2016 with Obama and former President George W. Bush, patron Oprah Winfrey and founding director Lonnie G. Bunch III. *The Washington Post* proclaimed it "the crown jewel" among the 19 Smithsonian museums. In recognition of Bunch's achievement, he was named Secretary of the Smithsonian, the first African American to hold the highest position among the nation's museums.

Artifacts that Bunch has collected for the museum include Emmett Till's 1955 casket, lunch counter stools from 1960 Greensboro sit-ins, Abraham Lincoln's 1863 Emancipation Proclamation, a Tuskegee Airmen 1944 Stearman PT-13D Kaydet, a Jim Crow-era railroad car for "Whites" and "colored," an early 19th-century slave cabin from South Carolina, a dress by seamstress Rosa Parks, the shawl that Queen Victoria sent Harriet Tubman, Oprah Winfrey's television studio couch, and Chuck Berry's 1973 red Cadillac convertible. Designed by the African American architectural group Freelon Adjaye Bond, the museum resembles a Yoruba crown, with three tiers of gleaming bronze lattice. Some 2 million visitors a year invest hours absorbing the exhibits and their stories.

Placard from March on Washington

LINCOLN MEMORIAL

The March on Washington for Jobs and Freedom began at the Washington Monument and culminated at the Lincoln Memorial on Aug. 28, 1963. One of the largest rallies for human rights in U.S. history, the march attracted approximately 250,000 people, with millions more watching television broadcasts around the world. Dr. King delivered his iconic "I Have a Dream" speech standing in front of the monument.

WE MARCH FOR EFFECTIVE CIVIL RIGHTS LAWS NOW

An estimated 250,000 activists stood together in peaceful protest against employment discrimination and other inequities.

The Lincoln Memorial, erected in honor of the U.S. president who issued the Emancipation Proclamation in 1863, rang with the words of another visionary a century later as Dr. King proclaimed, "I have a dream."

NATIONAL MUSEUM OF AFRICAN AMERICAN HISTORY & CULTURE

The National Museum of African American History and Culture houses tens of thousands of artifacts, many on display. In addition to recounting Black history, the Smithsonian's newest museum features exhibits on African American popular culture, illuminating contributions to the arts, music, comedy, fashion, literature, athletics and much more. After exiting the emotional galleries, visitors may reflect by a cascading waterfall in the Contemplative Court. The area features quotations by famous African Americans.

In the first half of the 19th century, the enslaved on Edisto Island, South Carolina, built the clapboard-covered Point of Pines Plantation cabin prominently displayed in the "Slavery and Freedom" exhibit. During the Civil War, African Americans on the Sea Islands "self-emancipated" two years before President Abraham Lincoln issued his proclamation in January 1863.

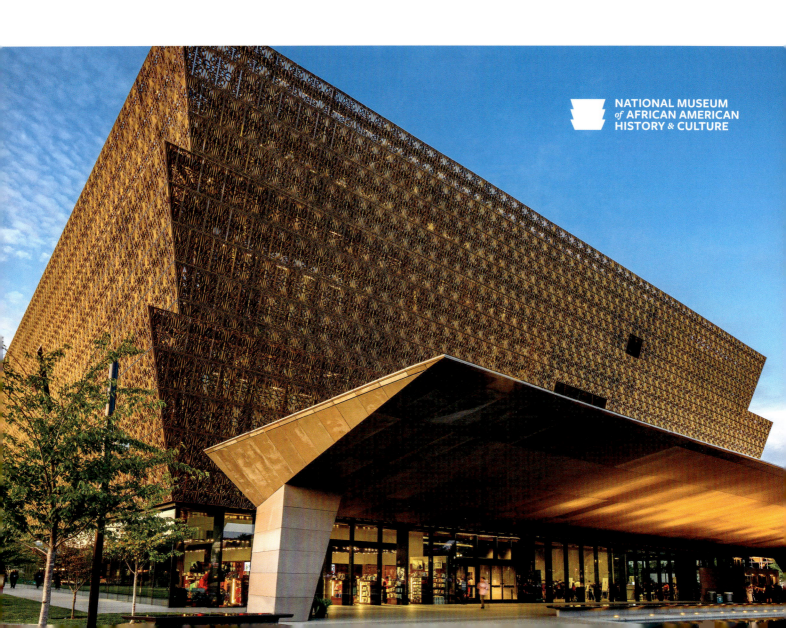

Point of Pines Cabin

MARTIN LUTHER KING JR. MEMORIAL

Dr. King was the first African American to be honored with a memorial on the National Mall. The monument captures the unwavering faith, strength and leadership of the nation's greatest civil rights leader through two massive granite structures – the "Stone of Hope" hewn from the "Mountain of Despair."

SUPREME COURT OF THE UNITED STATES

Among the many landmark rulings issued in the U.S. Supreme Court Building, perhaps none proved as far-reaching as *Brown v. Board of Education*, which found legal White supremacy unconstitutional. The decision overturned the "separate but equal" justification for maintaining segregation and resulted in the integration of public facilities from schools to bus stations across the country. When in session, the Supreme Court justices allow visitors into the building's courtroom on a first-come, first-served basis.

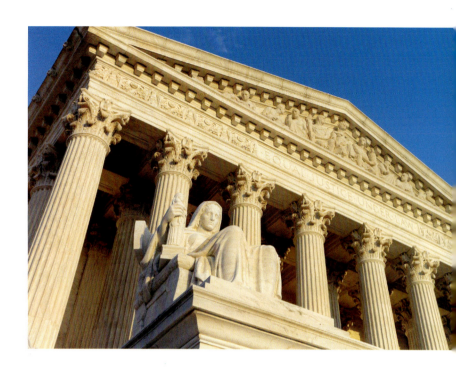

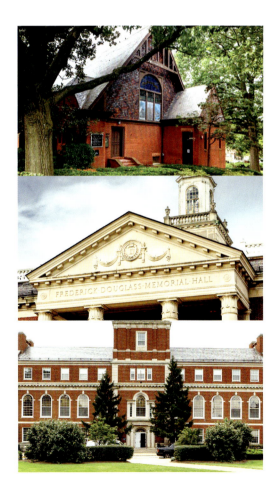

HOWARD UNIVERSITY:
ANDREW RANKIN MEMORIAL CHAPEL, FREDERICK DOUGLASS MEMORIAL HALL, FOUNDERS LIBRARY

These three buildings on the Yard at Howard University mark where School of Law Dean Charles Hamilton Houston and Thurgood Marshall developed the strategy of the NAACP Legal Defense and Educational Fund. Their efforts led to the overturning of the "separate but equal" lie of *Plessy v. Ferguson* by convincing the U.S. Supreme Court in *Brown v. Board of Education* to declare legal racial segregation unconstitutional.

1965

SELMA
ALABAMA

An estimated 600 Black people protesting for voting rights silently marched through the streets of Selma and over the Edmund Pettus Bridge toward Montgomery only to be tear-gassed and brutally beaten with billy clubs by Alabama state troopers. It was March 7, 1965, a day etched in history books as Bloody Sunday. After months of fierce White resistance to Black voter registration, the civil rights activists had mobilized in response to the murder of a Black man by a White officer.

Three weeks earlier on Feb. 18 in Marion some 23 miles into the countryside, 500 Black people holding a nighttime rally in support of jailed activist James Orange were confronted by dozens of armed state troopers dispatched by Gov. George Wallace to disrupt the protest. Shooting out streetlights, the troopers attacked the nonviolent demonstrators. Jimmie Lee Jackson, a 26-year-old Baptist deacon, tried to protect his mother and 82-year-old grandfather by seeking shelter in Mack's Café located behind Zion United Methodist Church. When Jackson attempted to shield his family, a trooper shot the young man in the stomach and he died eight days later in a Selma hospital. A *Montgomery Advertiser* editorial titled "Marion Massacre" decried, "It cannot be explained away by excuses because of 'outside agitators,' or provocation, which was present. It is the inside agitators in uniform who have disgraced Alabama." During Jackson's funeral, activist James Bevel vowed to organize a march from Selma to Montgomery and confront the governor over the unprovoked attack. It would make history.

On March 7, John Lewis of the Student Nonviolent Coordinating Committee and Hosea Williams of the Southern Christian Leadership Conference led marchers two columns abreast out of the Black community and through downtown over the bridge that crosses the Alabama River toward the state capital. Without provocation, state troopers — described by Lewis as a "sea of blue" — suddenly assaulted the peaceful marchers with weapons and tear gas. One trooper struck Lewis on the head, causing a concussion. "I thought I was going to die," he said. Another beat unconscious Selma's voter registration matriarch Amelia Boynton, 54, who was among 17 others hospitalized that day. (In 1958, the arrest of Boynton's son Bruce for challenging segregation in Richmond's bus station café resulted in the U.S. Supreme Court's 1960 *Boynton v. Virginia* decision. It ruled segregated interstate transit unconstitutional and led to the Freedom Rides.)

That evening, the national networks flashed across television screens footage of the state's brutal assault against nonviolent Black protestors in Selma, horrifying millions and leading legislators to call for new federal protections. Having secured the Civil

Jimmie Lee Jackson

An Alabama state trooper clubbed march leader John Lewis on Bloody Sunday, causing a concussion.

Rights Act of 1964 and anxious to move forward with voting rights legislation, President Lyndon B. Johnson addressed the U.S. Congress eight days after Bloody Sunday in a televised speech seen by 70 million Americans. "It is the effort of American Negroes to secure for themselves the full blessings of American life. Their cause must be our cause too. Because it is not just Negroes, but really it is all of us, who must overcome the crippling legacy of bigotry and injustice. And we shall overcome." Montgomery federal Judge Frank M. Johnson Jr., who a decade earlier sided with Rosa Parks against segregated seating on city buses, granted Dr. Martin Luther King Jr.'s request for federal protection of a march along the 54-mile journey. The judge lectured representatives of Gov. Wallace, saying, "What happened in Selma was an American tragedy. It is wrong to do violence to peaceful citizens in the streets of their own town."

On March 21 – two weeks after Bloody Sunday – Dr. King and his wife, Coretta Scott King, led the third march, which Lewis described as "a holy crusade, like Gandhi's march to the sea. It was no ordinary march. To me, there was never a march like this one before, and there hasn't been one since." Once the marchers reached the outskirts of Montgomery five days later, singer-actor Harry Belafonte hosted a "Stars for Freedom" concert at the City of St. Jude. The event featured Sammy Davis Jr., Tony Bennett, Joan Baez, Leonard Bernstein, Nina Simone and Dr. King's close friend Mahalia Jackson. The next day, March 26, the group of 3,000 that had left Selma was now – upon reaching Montgomery – 25,000 strong and stretched from the front of the Alabama Capitol down past Dexter Avenue Baptist Church from which Dr. King had led the Montgomery Bus Boycott 10 years before. In his "How Long, Not Long" speech, he thundered, "Let us march on ballot boxes until race-baiters disappear from the political arena." Gov. Wallace peeked through the blinds from his office and stayed silent.

The years of struggle for the vote in Alabama, Mississippi and across the South paid off five months later in August when the U.S. Congress passed the Voting Rights Act of 1965 with a vote of 328-74 in the House and 79-18 in the Senate. The law banned such voter suppression tactics as literacy and interpretation requirements, gerrymandered districts and other efforts to limit Black political empowerment. President Johnson smiled as he presented Dr. King with a signing pen.

In Marion, voters elected Perry County's first Black district attorney, Michael Jackson, and he indicted former state trooper James Bonard Fowler, who pled guilty to manslaughter for the murder of Jimmie Lee Jackson. Interestingly, three of the movement's leading women all hailed from Perry County: Coretta Scott King, Juanita Jones Abernathy and Jean Childs Young.

In 2013, the U.S. Supreme Court ruled 5-4 in the *Shelby County, Alabama v. Holder* decision to gut the 1965 Voting Rights Act's important preclearance enforcement provisions required of states with histories of racial discrimination in voting. A 2020 study by the Brennan Center for Justice found that the jurisdictions previously supervised by the Department of Justice – following removal of federal oversight by *Shelby* – had purged from the electorate hundreds of thousands of registered voters. Citing false claims of voter fraud, these state legislatures adopted new obstacles designed to limit access to the ballot, leading others to call for a new voting rights act.

When President Barack Obama celebrated the 50th anniversary of Bloody Sunday in Selma, he held the hand of Amelia Boynton who, at age 104, crossed the Edmund Pettus Bridge in a wheelchair. John Lewis said that day, "It was the killing of Jimmie Lee Jackson that provoked the march from Selma to Montgomery. It was his death and his blood that gave us the Voting Rights Act of 1965." Lewis hosted congressional delegations on Faith & Politics Institute pilgrimages to Alabama for more than 20 years until shortly before his death in 2020. During a weeklong tribute honoring Lewis's service to the nation, a horse-drawn carriage bearing his casket crossed the Edmund Pettus Bridge one last time.

Judge Frank M. Johnson Jr.

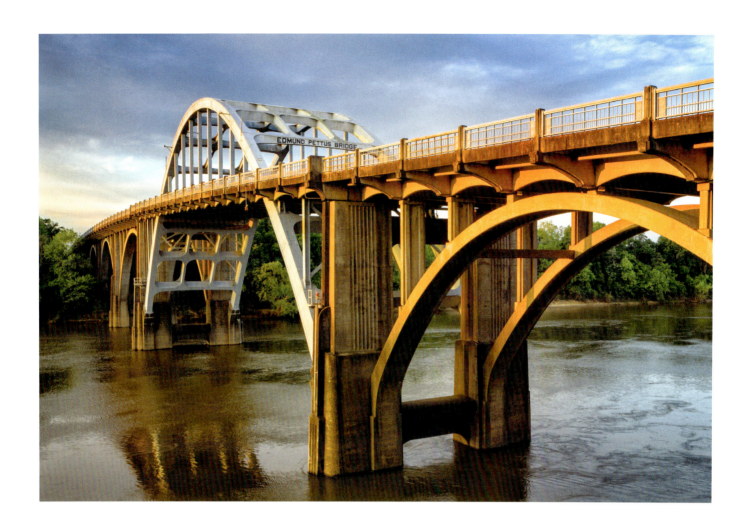

EDMUND PETTUS BRIDGE

On March 7, 1965, Alabama state troopers and Dallas County sheriff's deputies brutally assaulted 600 nonviolent Black demonstrators crossing the Edmund Pettus Bridge en route to the Capitol in Montgomery. ABC television news coverage of what became known as Bloody Sunday interrupted a network showing of the 1961 courtroom drama *Judgment at Nuremberg* that highlighted the brutality of Nazi soldiers on German citizens during World War II. Some 48 million people watching the movie then saw actual violence against American citizens seeking the right to vote. The irony that the Selma bridge was named for a former U.S. senator who had been a leader of the Ku Klux Klan was not lost on the marchers. The National Park Service's Selma Interpretive Center is housed in a three-story building near the bridge at the intersection of Water Avenue and Broad Street. The best view of the bridge is a block downriver at the 55-room St. James Hotel built in 1837 and reopened by Hilton in 2021. In the mid-1800s, Benjamin Sterling Turner was the enslaved manager of the hotel, which belonged to his owner, James Gee. Turner went on to become a successful businessman in Selma. After the Civil War, he bought the hotel and won election during Reconstruction as Alabama's first Black member of the U.S. House of Representatives.

Marchers crossed the Edmund Pettus Bridge en route to Montgomery.

The Edmund Pettus Bridge remains a symbol of the courageous stand for voting rights.

BROWN CHAPEL AME CHURCH

Civil rights activists assembled inside Brown Chapel AME as well as nearby First Baptist on March 7, 1965, prior to marching down Sylvan (now called Martin Luther King Street) to the commercial strip of Water Avenue, turning on Broad Street and heading over the Edmund Pettus Bridge. Led by John Lewis of the Student Nonviolent Coordinating Committee and Hosea Williams of the Southern Christian Leadership Conference and lined up side by side, the young and old Black protesters knelt in prayer when ordered to stop. "Troopers advance," came the cry as masked lawmen lobbed tear gas at the nonviolent demonstrators and then surged forward swinging nightsticks as marchers fled back across the bridge. A makeshift cavalry of county deputies used bullwhips and electric cattle prods to route the protesters down the street. The White officials even followed the demonstrators back into their churches, beating them there.

LOWNDES INTERPRETIVE CENTER & SELMA TO MONTGOMERY NATIONAL HISTORIC TRAIL

Congress authorized the 54-mile route from Selma to Montgomery as a National Historic Trail in 1996. In the third and successful march attempt that began March 21, 1965, Dr. King and his wife, Coretta Scott King, led activists from Selma's Brown Chapel over the Edmund Pettus Bridge, through Lowndes County and into Montgomery. The National Park Service operates three visitor centers along the route. The Lowndes County Interpretive Center in White Hall is midway and the largest of the three. Its architecture reflects a stylized version of the Brown Chapel Church façade and the arch of the Edmund Pettus Bridge. Because U.S. 80 narrowed to only two lanes in Lowndes County, U.S. District Judge Frank Johnson Jr. set a limit of 300 participants during that portion of the route. In addition to commemorating the "tent city" previously erected on the site by Black sharecroppers evicted for supporting voting rights, the center memorializes the two White martyrs murdered in Lowndes County: Viola Liuzzo, a Detroit housewife and Tennessee native shot by Klansmen while driving a Black man in her car back to Selma along Highway 80 after the march, and Jonathan Daniels, an Episcopal seminarian from New Hampshire shot for promoting race reform in Hayneville.

The Selma Interpretive Center is at the northwest approach to the bridge. The Montgomery Interpretive Center is on the campus of Alabama State University and chronicles Dr. King's remarks during the celebrity-filled "Stars of Freedom" rally organized by singer-actor Harry Belafonte to entertain the marchers. Dr. King delivered his "How Long, Not Long" speech the following day in front of the Capitol in Montgomery.

PRESIDENT BARACK OBAMA

'For we were born of change'

Then-President Barack Obama gave the following remarks on the occasion of the 50th anniversary of the Selma-to-Montgomery March. His address has been condensed for brevity.

"There are places and moments in America where this nation's destiny has been decided. Many are sites of war – Concord and Lexington, Appomattox, Gettysburg. Others are sites that symbolize the daring of America's character – Independence Hall and Seneca Falls, Kitty Hawk and Cape Canaveral. Selma is such a place.

"In one afternoon 50 years ago, so much of our turbulent history – the stain of slavery and anguish of civil war; the yoke of segregation and tyranny of Jim Crow; the death of four little girls in Birmingham; and the dream of a Baptist preacher – all that history met on this bridge.

"It was not a clash of armies, but a clash of wills; a contest to determine the true meaning of America. And because of men and women like John Lewis, Joseph Lowery, Hosea Williams, Amelia Boynton, Diane Nash, Ralph Abernathy, C.T. Vivian, Andrew Young, Fred Shuttlesworth, Dr. Martin Luther King Jr. and so many others, the idea of a just America and a fair America, an inclusive America, and a generous America – that idea ultimately triumphed. In time, their chorus would well up and reach President Johnson. And he would send them protection, and speak to the nation, echoing their call for America and the world to hear: 'We shall overcome.' What enormous faith these men and women had. Faith in God, but also faith in America.

"That's why Selma is not some outlier in the American experience. That's why it's not a museum or a static monument to behold from a distance. It is instead the manifestation of a creed written into our founding documents: 'We the people ... in order to form a more perfect union.' 'We hold these truths to be self-evident, that all men are created equal.' Because of campaigns like this [the Selma-to-Montgomery

March], a Voting Rights Act was passed. Political and economic and social barriers came down. And the change these men and women wrought is visible here today in the presence of African Americans who run boardrooms, who sit on the bench, who serve in elected office from small towns to big cities; from the Congressional Black Caucus all the way to the Oval Office.

"The Voting Rights Act was one of the crowning achievements of our democracy, the result of Republican and Democratic efforts. President Reagan signed its renewal when he was in office. President George W. Bush signed its renewal when he was in office. One hundred members of Congress have come here today to honor people who were willing to die for the right to protect it. If we want to honor this day, let that hundred go back to Washington and gather 400 more, and together, pledge to make it their mission to restore that law this year. That's how we honor those on this bridge.

"We are Sojourner Truth and Fannie Lou Hamer, women who could do as much as any man and then some. And we're Susan B. Anthony, who shook the system until the law reflected that truth. That is our character. And that's what the young people here today and listening all across the country must take away from this day. You are America. Unconstrained by habit and convention. Unencumbered by what is, because you're ready to seize what ought to be.

"Because Selma shows us that America is not the project of any one person. Because the single-most powerful word in our democracy is the word 'We.' 'We the people.' 'We shall overcome.' 'Yes, we can.' That word is owned by no one. It belongs to everyone. Oh, what a glorious task we are given, to continually try to improve this great nation of ours.

"Fifty years from Bloody Sunday, our march is not yet finished, but we're getting closer. Two hundred and thirty-nine years after this nation's founding our union is not yet perfect, but we are getting closer. Our job's easier because somebody already got us through that first mile. Somebody already got us over that bridge. When it feels the road is too hard, when the torch we've been passed feels too heavy, we will remember these early travelers, and draw strength from their example, and hold firmly the words of the prophet Isaiah: 'Those who hope in the Lord will renew their strength. They will soar on wings like eagles. They will run and not grow weary. They will walk and not be faint.'"

President Barack Obama led the way across the Edmund Pettus Bridge on March 7, 2015, the 50th anniversary of the Selma-to-Montgomery March.

1968

MEMPHIS
TENNESSEE

For months, Memphis garbage collectors had complained about unsafe working conditions and pay so low that employees with 40-hour-a-week jobs still qualified for welfare and food stamps. Then on Feb. 1, 1968, a malfunctioning compactor crushed to death African Americans Robert Walker and Echol Cole. Two weeks later, union organizer T.O. Jones led the 1,300 employees in the Memphis Department of Public Works out on strike over dangerous conditions and unfair wages. The city backtracked on an agreement to recognize the union and responded to a protest march on Feb. 23 with police suppression as White officers sprayed the faces of Black demonstrators with mace. What began as a unionization drive quickly became a civil rights campaign. Led by the Rev. James Lawson — whose workshops on nonviolence had trained movement activists in Nashville and elsewhere and who now pastored Centenary Church in Memphis — the strike's demand for a livable wage summarized the shift the movement had taken.

By 1967, Dr. Martin Luther King Jr. had begun to emphasize the "triple evils of racism, militarism and poverty." He understood how a coalition of labor and civil rights leaders had secured the Civil Rights Act of 1964 and the Voting Rights Act of 1965, which tackled legal White supremacy, and he wanted to focus the coalition's attention on the unresolved issue of economic justice. Through the Southern Christian Leadership Conference (SCLC), Dr. King proposed a Poor People's Campaign in which working-class Americans of all races would occupy Washington, D.C., until Congress addressed systemic inequality. Seeing Memphis as a microcosm of the struggle and aware of the SCLC's plans, Lawson invited his old comrade to town.

With an electricity that recalled earlier moments in the struggles of the bus boycott, sit-ins and marches, some 25,000 people packed the Mason Temple Church of God in Christ to hear Dr. King speak on March 18, 1968. For over a month, the strike had waged on with Lawson preaching to the devalued workers, "You are human beings. You are men. You deserve dignity." Signs printed for the picket line read "I AM A MAN." The night of March 18, Dr. King warmed up to his audience, saying, "All labor has dignity." He urged unity with "We can get more organized together than we can apart." And he called for a work stoppage to show the power of mobilized Black people.

Placard from sanitation workers strike

Civil rights leader Dr. Martin Luther King Jr. collapsed on the balcony of the Lorraine Motel, fatally wounded by an assassin's bullet.

On the morning of March 28, a cross-section of Black Memphians, from garbage collectors to schoolchildren, domestic workers to professionals, gathered outside the strike headquarters at Clayborn Temple AME Church, all united in a general strike. Dr. King joined Lawson and 15,000 people singing "We Shall Overcome" as the march began. On Beale Street, the nonviolent movement confronted heightened racial tension, for among the thousands of teenagers, some – inspired by Black Power rhetoric – began breaking windows. Long pent-up anger resulted in a riot, and then looting. Absent at the start, now hostile White police blocked the marchers at Main Street. Halting, Lawson turned the procession around as masked officers, firing tear gas into the crowd, charged with clubs and mace, targeting strike leaders for beatings. Exerting nonviolent discipline, Lawson sent Dr. King to safety and escorted the rest back to Clayborn Temple, but police followed, entering the sanctuary, spraying tear gas and clubbing refugees.

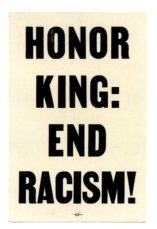

The march lay bare Black America's dilemma: whether to support nonviolence or embrace rebellion in the face of continued resistance to racial justice. Blaming Dr. King, critics suggested violence would occur in Washington during the Poor People's Campaign. Dr. King knew he had to return and march to demonstrate the efficacy of nonviolence.

Tornadoes threatened Memphis on April 3 as an exhausted Dr. King emerged from the rain and thunder and entered Mason Temple where strike supporters had gathered. Lawson and the Rev. Ralph Abernathy readied the crowd. Fear from constant death threats receded and fatigue dissipated in the warm embrace Dr. King received from his receptive audience. Destiny marked the evening as he delivered an extemporaneous address ringing with emotion. He emphasized that the greatest change already had occurred internally when Black people stood up to White supremacy. He recounted the successes from the Montgomery Bus Boycott to Birmingham, Selma and now Memphis, adding, "We've got to see it through." Foreshadowing the morrow, a transcendent Dr. King, tears in his eyes and a tremble in his voice, ended his impassioned speech with "And I've *seen* the Promised Land. I may not get there with you. But I want you to know tonight that we, as a people, will get to the Promised Land. And I'm happy tonight. I'm not worried about anything. I'm not fearing any man!"

Under segregation, Black travelers relied on the *Green Book* to suggest lodging, identifying in Memphis the Lorraine Motel owned by Walter and Loree Bailey, which provided accommodations to such upscale A-listers as Aretha Franklin, Ray Charles and Jackie Robinson. On this return, Dr. King checked into Room 306 with 307 reserved for SCLC use. Preparing to depart for dinner early in the evening of April 4, Dr. King stood on the motor court balcony speaking to his lieutenants in the parking lot below: Andrew Young, Hosea Williams, James Bevel, Bernard Lee and Jesse Jackson. He called to saxophonist Ben Branch to play "Precious Lord" at the mass meeting scheduled for Mason Temple.

The previous January, a Missouri prison escapee, White supremacist and habitual thief named James Earl Ray had begun scouring newspapers for coverage of Dr. King's travels. He wanted to become a famous fugitive and have actor Efrem Zimbalist Jr. brand him "most wanted" at the conclusion of the Sunday night TV show "The FBI." While staying at a Birmingham, Alabama, boardinghouse at 2806 Highland Avenue, Ray purchased a 1966 white Ford Mustang with 18,000 miles for $1,995, and a Remington Gamemaster .30-06 pump-action rifle. He followed Dr. King to Memphis on April 3 and saw media coverage of

Placard held by mourners

the Black preacher standing in front of Room 306 at the Lorraine Motel. Ray located the motel and determined that a two-story rooming house that overlooked the Lorraine across Mulberry Street offered adequate surveillance.

As Dr. King turned on the motel balcony, a shot rang out, piercing the apostle of nonviolence who collapsed onto the concrete as Abernathy, his best friend, emerged from Room 306. When police reached the scene, movement leaders pointed to the nearby boardinghouse as the source of the gunfire. Evidence found there implicated Ray in the murder.

Four days later, the martyred leader's widow, Coretta Scott King, and their children led 42,000 people in a silent — and nonviolent — march through Memphis streets. Two weeks later, the strike ended as the city recognized the garbage collectors' union and increased their pay. One month later, Abernathy and Dr. King's lieutenants entered Washington as the Poor People's Campaign erected Resurrection City near the Lincoln Memorial and peaceably occupied government buildings, demanding economic justice.

In 1976, at the urging of Mrs. King and others, Congress established a House Select Committee on Assassinations. The investigation reported in July 1979 that James Earl Ray "knowingly, intelligently and voluntarily pleaded guilty" on March 10, 1969, but also that he alone "fired one shot at Dr. Martin Luther King Jr. The shot killed Dr. King."

Memphis sanitation workers went on strike in protest of dangerous working conditions and poor wages.

NATIONAL CIVIL RIGHTS MUSEUM AT THE LORRAINE MOTEL

After Dr. King's assassination, pilgrims began visiting the Lorraine and rooms 306 and 307, which the motel's owners kept vacant as shrines. But otherwise, the business struggled and eventually transitioned to residential housing. Later foreclosed on, the motel was purchased by Black activists to save it from demolition. Money from state, local and federal governments as well as private sources restored the façade and created within the motel the National Civil Rights Museum, which opened in 1991 as the country's first such facility. Today, 350,000 visitors a year pass by the Lorraine's iconic and colorful ultramodern sign to begin their tour of the African American freedom struggle and the story of the movement and Memphis.

CLAYBORN TEMPLE

Originally constructed by White Presbyterians but later bought by a Black African Methodist Episcopal congregation, Clayborn Temple served as the headquarters for the striking garbage collectors in 1968. Distributed from here, the "I AM A MAN" placard with its assertion of self-determination and rejection of demeaning White supremacy became the symbol of the Memphis movement. As the demonstration ended in disarray March 28, police stormed Clayborn Temple, firing tear gas into the sanctuary and beating nonviolent protesters seeking refuge there.

MASON TEMPLE CHURCH OF GOD IN CHRIST

Thousands packed Memphis's largest Black auditorium, the Mason Temple Church of God in Christ, on a stormy night, April 3, 1968, to hear what would be Dr. King's last public speech. Having returned to prove the power of nonviolence and support the strikers, he warned that no longer was the "choice between violence and nonviolence in this world, it's nonviolence or nonexistence." With overwhelming emotion, Dr. King declared, "I've been to the mountaintop," the name given to his final address.

1968

ATLANTA
GEORGIA

From the pulpit of Ebenezer Baptist Church, Dr. Martin Luther King Jr. preached his own eulogy two months to the day before his assassination in Memphis. The Atlanta native was back in the church of his father and grandfather, a place foundational to his development as a pastor and civil rights leader. Today, the historic church is part of the Martin Luther King Jr. National Historical Park along famed Auburn Avenue, as is Dr. King's birth home, his gravesite at the King Center for Nonviolent Social Change, and the Visitor Center with its interpretive exhibits maintained by the National Park Service.

As the second pastor of the congregation, the Rev. A.D. Williams – Dr. King's grandfather – built the historic Ebenezer Baptist Church in 1914. By then, Atlanta's enforcement of urban segregation had attracted the Black middle class to "Sweet Auburn," which became one of the richest Black neighborhoods in the country. Williams bought from a German immigrant the 1895 Victorian house at 501 Auburn Avenue and raised a daughter there, Alberta. She married the Rev. Martin Luther King Sr., an ambitious preacher who joined her father in the pulpit at Ebenezer. Three children were born to Alberta and "Daddy King": A.D.W. King, Christine King (Farris) and, on Jan. 15, 1929, Martin Luther King Jr.

Growing up in the church and attending Morehouse College exposed the youngest King to global struggles for racial justice and prepared him for a life in the ministry. After attending Crozer Theological Seminary and then Boston University, he completed his Ph.D. while pastoring Dexter Avenue Baptist Church in Montgomery, Alabama. Joining Bayard Rustin and others who wanted to marshal the momentum of the successful Montgomery Bus Boycott into a regional movement, Dr. King called for activist Black ministers to gather at Ebenezer in January 1957 to organize the Southern Christian Leadership Conference (SCLC).

Growing responsibilities as president of the SCLC – with its headquarters in Atlanta's Prince Hall Masonic Building on Auburn

Dr. Martin Luther King Jr.

Dr. King served as co-pastor with his father, "Daddy King," at Ebenezer Baptist Church on Auburn Avenue.

Avenue – led Dr. King to resign his pulpit at Dexter and accept a co-pastorate with his father at Ebenezer in January 1960. He moved with wife Coretta Scott King and their two children, M.L. King III and Yolanda, to a house on Boulevard. Two more children, Bernice and Dexter, were born in Atlanta. From here, Dr. King led the SCLC's response to the sit-ins, Freedom Rides and demonstrations in Albany, Birmingham, Selma and Memphis.

Pastoral obligations interspersed his civil rights activism as he gained solace and strength from the Atlanta community in the face of mounting criticism over his stance against the war in Vietnam and plans for the Poor People's Campaign. The movement had splintered between advocates of nonviolence and integration and others demanding Black Power and separatism. At the onset of the garbage collectors' strike on Feb. 4, 1968, a weary and burdened Dr. King preached from the pulpit of Ebenezer a sermon called "The Drum Major Instinct." In it, he offered his own eulogy: "I'd like somebody to mention that day that Martin Luther King Jr. tried to give his life serving others … tried to love somebody … to be right on the war question … to feed the hungry … to clothe those who were naked … to visit those who were in prison … to love and serve humanity."

A devastated Black community in Atlanta received Dr. King's body following his murder in Memphis, holding the funeral at Ebenezer Baptist Church. Thousands came to view the martyr's remains prior to the service at which was played a recording of his final sermon with its call to be "a drum major for righteousness." A cotton wagon carrying the coffin and pulled by Gee's Bend mules led a procession of 100,000 people past the Georgia Capitol ringed by hostile, riot-helmeted state troopers and to Morehouse College where Mahalia Jackson sang "Precious Lord" during a second open-air funeral before burial in South View Cemetery.

Ordained at age 19, Dr. King followed in the footsteps of his father and maternal grandfather in ministry to the congregation at Ebenezer Baptist Church.

EBENEZER BAPTIST CHURCH

Generations of the King family have led Ebenezer Baptist Church where Martin Luther King Jr. was baptized, ordained and served as co-pastor. In 1999, the congregation moved into a new sanctuary across Auburn Avenue so that the National Park Service could restore the historic building and conduct tours of the sanctuary in which plays a recording of "The Drum Major Instinct." From Ebenezer's new pulpit emerged Savannah native Raphael Warnock who, in 2021, became the first African American from Georgia to win election to the U.S. Senate.

MARTIN LUTHER KING JR. NATIONAL HISTORICAL PARK

Included in the Martin Luther King Jr. National Historical Park are Dr. King's birth home, Ebenezer Baptist Church, the King Center with the gravesite of Dr. and Mrs. King, the National Park Service (NPS) bookstore, and the Southern Christian Leadership Conference offices in the Prince Hall Masonic Building. In addition to parking and restrooms, the NPS Visitor Center has six interpretive pods that tell the life of the King family on Auburn Avenue and the course of the Civil Rights Movement. There is also a statue of Mahatma Gandhi at the start of the original International Civil Rights Walk of Fame, which displays footprints of activists.

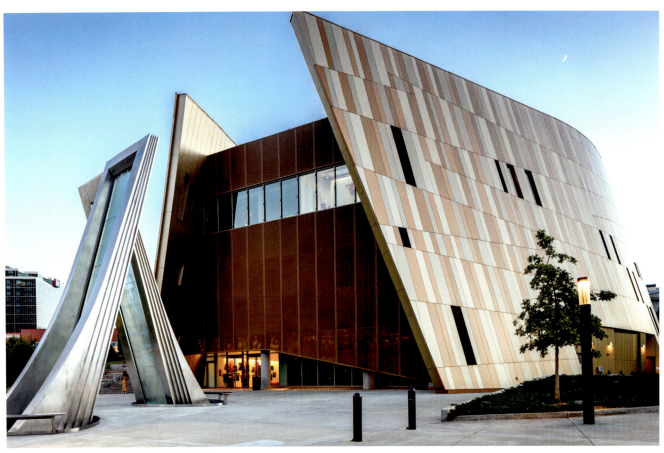

NATIONAL CENTER FOR CIVIL & HUMAN RIGHTS

Located off Auburn Avenue at Centennial Olympic Park, Atlanta's National Center for Civil and Human Rights features multisensory exhibits exploring the history of the Civil Rights Movement within the context of global struggles for freedom. A collection of Benny Andrews paintings tells the John Lewis story. Choice items from the King Papers purchased by the city and housed at the Atlanta University Woodruff Library are in constant rotation so as to display a variety of historic documents. The International Civil Rights Walk of Fame, first established at the Martin Luther King Jr. National Historical Park Visitor Center, is continued here.

Historic Ebenezer Baptist Church is part of the National Park Service and is open to the public.

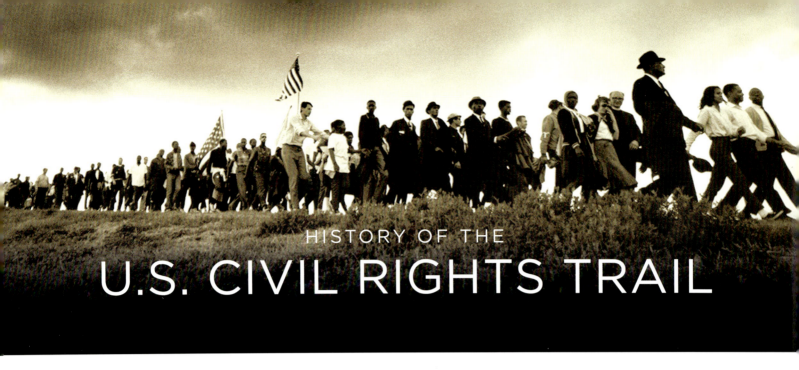

HISTORY OF THE
U.S. CIVIL RIGHTS TRAIL

When jailed with hundreds of others in 1963 for protesting segregation, Dr. Martin Luther King Jr. wrote, "One day the South will recognize its real heroes."

But for two decades after the Civil Rights Movement came to a close with Dr. King's death in 1968, the public showed little interest in the sites where Black foot soldiers had defeated legal segregation in the South. In 1984, Alabama tourism director Ed Hall published the *Black Heritage Guide*, the first state-sponsored publication of its kind, and his department regularly expanded it for the next 20 years.

With the growing restoration of civil rights landmarks and opening of civil rights museums in Alabama, subsequent state tourism director Lee Sentell evolved the guide into the Alabama Civil Rights Trail. *The Washington Post* published a major feature on Feb. 22, 2009, that noted "Alabama bears the scars of the civil rights era, and the monuments to that struggle inspire the courage to face new challenges." Others took notice. When the Dalai Lama toured the Birmingham Civil Rights District in 2014, Sentell presented His Holiness with a miniature sculpture of Rosa Parks seated on a bus bench.

President Barack Obama instructed the National Park Service to create more diversity among the nation's few UNESCO World Heritage sites, with particular interest in civil rights. At Alabama's request in 2016, a Georgia State University team led by Glenn T. Eskew researched and identified 60 civil rights landmarks as potential UNESCO candidates.

Southern state tourism departments, working together as the Atlanta-based Travel South USA trade association, added more sites and formed a parallel U.S. Civil Rights Trail as the university moved forward on the potential World Heritage nomination. Work on the trail began in 2017 when Ed Mizzell, managing director of Luckie & Company advertising agency, selected former *Southern Living* photographer Art Meripol to visit and capture new images of movement landmarks. Luckie graphic designer Miles Wright then designed CivilRightsTrail.com, which logged more than a million pageviews soon after the website launched on Martin Luther King Jr. Day in 2018.

The ad agency produced a campaign under the theme *"What happened here changed the world."* It demonstrated that scores of the movement's landmarks were open for tours. One ad featured an iconic image of protestors staging a sit-in at the Greensboro Woolworth in 1960. The headline read, "See where they took a seat to make a stand." *TIME* magazine upgraded placement of the ad, moving it to the inside front cover for all 2 million copies. When the cover story of a 2018 issue of *Smithsonian* magazine bannered "1968: The Year That Shattered America," the Civil Rights Trail ran an ad in the magazine with a vintage photo showing voting-rights protesters crossing the Edmund Pettus Bridge in Selma. It suggested "Walk in the footsteps of giants." The campaign earned three national advertising awards.

Today, the trail links important Black churches, school museums, residences of courageous leaders, rural courthouses, and other landmarks and describes how descendants of enslaved people cast off social shackles to claim their rightful roles as American citizens as promised by the Constitution's 13th, 14th and 15th amendments.

The trail encompasses 20-plus museums and visitor centers operated by the National Park Service (NPS). More are in development. On Obama's last week in office in 2017, he conferred NPS designations to establish the Birmingham Civil Rights National Monument; the Freedom Riders National Monument in Anniston, Alabama; and the Reconstruction Era National Historical Park in Beaufort County, South Carolina. More recently, the home of Medgar Evers in Jackson, Mississippi, was designated the Medgar and Myrlie Evers Home National Monument.

Magazines and national newspapers have offered extensive coverage. On Dec. 3, 2017, *The New York Times* headlined "In the South and North, New (and Vital) Civil Rights Trails." When the first state-funded civil rights memorial opened in late 2017, the New York newspaper headlined "The New Mississippi Civil Rights Museum Refuses To Sugarcoat History." On Aug. 10, 2018, *The Times* ran three color pages, raving that "the new United States Civil Rights Trail is a rewarding starting point." The same day, *The Washington Post* devoted a full page to the Robert Russa Moton High School, a little-known but pivotal Virginia civil rights landmark. In 2019, *National Geographic Traveler* devoted 12 pages to a lengthy road trip selected as an "Epic Journey." In 2020, *Reader's Digest* published a 10-page feature translated into 21 languages for a total circulation of 10 million copies worldwide.

On April 20, 2018, *The Times* reported that "the current excitement surrounding civil rights tourism is expected to attract 5 million visitors who will spend some $725 million [in 2018]." Visitors responded by setting heritage tourism attendance records. In Washington, D.C., the Smithsonian's National Museum of African American History and Culture attracts more than 2 million visitors a year. In Atlanta, the Martin Luther King Jr. National Historical Park and the King Center host in excess of a million guests on major anniversary years, with that number expected in 2023, the 55th anniversary of Dr. King's death.

In Memphis, the National Civil Rights Museum receives more than 350,000 visitors annually. The Mississippi Civil Rights Museum in Jackson exceeds attendance projections each year. In Montgomery, the National Memorial for Peace and Justice, established by Bryan Stevenson's Equal Justice Initiative to recognize the thousands of lynchings in the U.S., and its related museum drew 500,000 guests during the second year they were open.

In London, the International Travel & Tourism Awards named the U.S. Civil Rights Trail as Best Regional Destination Campaign the first year it was eligible. CNBC interviewed trail founder Lee Sentell and Liz Bittner, president of Travel South, about the trail's success.

The Smithsonian Institution and *The New York Times* were the first two national cultural organizations to sponsor escorted tours of the trail. International firms Abercrombie & Kent and Trafalgar Travel followed suit. Independent travelers use CivilRightsTrail.com to plan visits.

Hudson Group, one of North America's leading travel retailers, located its Civil Rights Trail Market at the Birmingham-Shuttlesworth International Airport between gates C1 and C2, offering biographies, postcards and guidebooks, including the *Moon U.S. Civil Rights Trail*, a highly detailed travel planner by award-winning journalist Deborah D. Douglas.

The Dalai Lama and Lee Sentell

SPECIAL ACKNOWLEDGMENT

Douglas Brinkley, Sharon Calcote, Kimberly Clay, Spencer Crew, Meredith DaSilva, Theodore Debro, Connie Dyson, Mary Elliott, Mark Ezell, Anne Farrisee, Elliott Ferguson, Judy Forte, Stephen Foutes, Gerold Frank, Mickie Goodson, Ed Hall, Cromwell Handy, Emily Hatfield, Logan Hildebrand, Meghan Hood, Bill Huie, Bridgette Jobe, Clarence B. Jones, Ryan M. Jones, Rosemary Judkins, Kevin Langston, Caroline Logan, Robin McClain, Rita McClenny, Carol McElheney, Dixie McPherson, Faith Morris, Stephen Morris, André Nabors, Travis Napper, Duane Parrish, Cam Patterson, Nekasha Pratt, Arthur Price, Kristine Puckett, Craig Ray, Joe David Rice, Chelsea Ruby, Hampton Sides, Lori Simms, Joseph E. Taff, Noelle Trent, Dana Young

For comments, email Sentell@civilrightstrail.com

Lee Sentell (left) heard Dr. Martin Luther King Jr. speak during the Selma march in 1965, which inspired him later as state tourism director to create the Alabama Civil Rights Trail. Alabama partnered with other Travel South states to develop the U.S. Civil Rights Trail in 2017, the year the state honored U.S. Rep. John Lewis with a historical marker, unveiled by Sentell and Nicklaus Chrysson as Lewis and his friend U.S. Rep. Terri Sewell of Selma looked on.